Joseph M. Williams

Style

Toward Clarity and Grace

With two chapters coauthored by
Gregory G. Colomb

The University of Chicago Press
Chicago and London

The University of Chicago Press, Chicago 60637
The University of Chicago Press, Ltd., London
Published by arrangement with Scott, Foresman and Company
Copyright © 1990 by Joseph M. Williams
Copyright © 1989, 1985, 1981 by Scott, Foresman and Company
All rights reserved. Published 1990
Paperback edition 1995
Printed in the United States of America

99 98 97   10 9 8

⊜ The paper used in this publication meets
the minimum requirements of the American National
Standard for Information Sciences—Permanence of
Paper for Printed Library Materials, ANSI Z39.48-1984.

Library of Congress Cataloging in Publication Data

Williams, Joseph M.
    Style : toward clarity and grace / Joseph M. Williams.
        p.   cm. — (Chicago guides to writing, editing, and
    publishing)
    Includes bibliographical references.

    ISBN 0-226-89915-2 (paper)
    1. English, language—Style.   I. Title.   II. Series.
PE1421.W546   1990
808'.042—dc20   90-34828
                                                CIP

. . . English style, familiar but not coarse, elegant but not ostentatious . . .

Samuel Johnson

Contents

Preface

This book originated as *Style,* first published as a textbook by Scott Foresman in 1981 and then in two more editions in 1985 and 1989. I wrote it for four reasons. First, the standard books on style don't go much beyond high mindedness. They are all for accuracy, brevity, clarity, and so forth, but beyond offering good and bad examples, none of them explains how to achieve those ends. Second, the standard books gesture toward audiences, but none of them explains in detail how a writer must anticipate what readers look for as they make their way through complex, usually unfamiliar material. Third, the standard books seem wholly innocent of recent work done in the cognitive sciences, much of it centrally relevant to understanding the problems that readers have to solve every time they begin a new sentence. And fourth, the standard handbooks mainly address belletristic or journalistic writing. None of them reflects sustained experience working with writers in areas other than literature or journalism. In *Style,* I tried to integrate research into the ways that readers read with my experience working with professional writing in a variety of fields, in order to create a system of principles that would simultaneously diagnose the quality of writing and, if necessary, suggest ways to improve it.

In 1988 the University of Chicago Press inquired whether *Style* might be revised for use outside a classroom. Since many readers had reported learning a good deal from reading *Style* on their own, a new version specifically for such an audience seemed to be a good idea.

The objective of this book remains the same: to explain how writers can improve the style and the structure of their reports, analyses, articles, memoranda, proposals, monographs, books. In Chapters 5 and 6, Gregory Colomb and I go beyond matters of sentence style to discuss larger matters of form and organization.

We do not directly address the kind of prose that some might call "imaginative" or "expressive." At some level, of course, all writers express feelings, all writers imagine, no sensible writer deliberately avoids turning a graceful phrase, no matter how banal the subject. Aesthetic pleasure and clarity are by no means mutually exclusive; indeed, they are usually part of the same experience. But the object of our attention is writing whose success we measure not primarily by the pleasure we derive from it, but by how well it does a job of work. If it also gives us a tingle of pleasure, so much the better.

Except for a page or two at the end of Chapter 6, we discuss neither how to prepare for nor how to produce a first draft. There is folk wisdom about what we ought to do—brainstorm, take notes, make a scratch outline, analyze objectives, define audiences; then as we draft, keep on writing, don't stop to revise minute details of punctuation, spelling, etc., let the act of writing generate ideas. When we create a first draft, we should be most concerned with getting onto the page something that reflects what we had in mind when we began to write and, if we are lucky, something new that we didn't.

But once we have made clear to ourselves what ideas, points, and arguments might be available, we then have to reshape that first draft to provide what our readers need. We write a first draft for ourselves; the drafts thereafter increasingly for the reader. That is the central objective of this book: to show how a writer quickly and efficiently transforms a rough first draft into a version crafted for the reader.

Two More Objectives

We set for ourselves two more objectives, because seeming clarity in professional writing is a matter that depends on more than merely a writer's level of skill. First, mature writers can write badly for different reasons—confusion about a subject, insufficient time to revise, carelessness, entrenched bad habits, sheer incompetence. But to casual readers, these causes may result in what seems to be the same kind of tangled prose. Those who experience problems with their writing have to understand that they must approach different causes of bad writing in different ways. That understanding is even more crucial to those who have to deal with the writing of others. So we explain how bad writing results from different causes and how writers can diagnose different problems and overcome them.

There is a second general objective: It is important for everyone—those who write professional prose and those who have to read it—to understand not only its social origins but its social consequences. When a piece of writing confuses us, we often assume that we are not up to its demands. Difficult a passage may be, but its complexity is often more seeming than substantial. We have seen hundreds of students experience relief from doubts about their own competence when they realize that if they are unable to understand an article or monograph, it is not necessarily because they are incompetent, but because its author couldn't write clearly. That liberation is a valuable experience.

Whether we are readers or writers, teachers or editors, all of us in professional communities must understand three things about complex writing:

- it may precisely reflect complex ideas,
- it may gratuitously complicate complex ideas,
- it may gratuitously complicate simple ideas.

Here is an example of the second kind of complexity:

> Similarities may develop in the social organization of societies at similar levels of economic development because there are "imperatives" built into the socio-technical system they adopt which drive them to similar responses to common problems. This model, therefore, places great emphasis on the level of economic development of nations to account for movement towards common forms of social organization. Alternatively, convergence may result from simple borrowing, so that a model of the diffusion of innovation becomes appropriate. Where such borrowing occurs levels of development may be less relevant than integration in networks of influence through which ideas and social forms are diffused. Economic development may, of course, set limits on the capacity of a nation to institute systems available to be copied, and the propensities to copy may enable nations to install convergent patterns more rapidly than one would have predicted from knowledge of their level of economic development.[1]

This means,

> Societies at similar levels of economic development may converge because "imperatives" in their sociotechnical system cause them to respond to similar problems in similar ways. To explain this,

the model emphasizes economic development. But societies may also converge because they borrow, so a model would have to explain how ideas and social forms diffuse through networks of influence. Of course, a society at a low level of development may be unable to copy features of some systems. But a society with a strong propensity to copy may do so more rapidly than predicted.

Here is an example of the third kind of complexity,

> The absence from this dictionary of a handful of old, well-known vulgate terms for sexual and excretory organs and functions is not due to a lack of citations for these words from current literature. On the contrary, the profusion of such citations in recent years would suggest that the terms in question are so well known as to require no explanation. The decision to eliminate them as part of the extensive culling process that is the inevitable task of the lexicographer was made on the practical grounds that there is still objection in many quarters to the appearance of these terms in print and that to risk keeping this dictionary out of the hands of some students by introducing several terms that require little if any elucidation would be unwise.
> —From the foreword, *Webster's New World Dictionary of the American Language*[2]

This means,

> We excluded vulgar words for sex and excretion not because we could not find them. We excluded them because many people object to seeing them. Had we included them, some teachers and schoolboards would have refused to let this dictionary be used by their students, who in any event already know what those words mean.

It is not always easy to distinguish these kinds of complexity. When we are not experts in a subject, we tend to doubt our own competence before we doubt a writer's. And so we defer to what seems difficult, often mistakenly. The immediate objective of this book is to help those who write about complex matters; its larger objective is to help those of us who have to read what they write.

Some Encouragement, Caveats, and Disclaimers

We believe that you will find here much that is familiar. What will seem new is the language we offer to articulate what you already know. That language will require some work. If you are nostalgically confident about having mastered the skills of parsing and diagramming, you should know that we have given some old terms new meanings. Moreover, a few readers comfortable with that traditional vocabulary may be disconcerted to find that they must learn new terms for new concepts. Many believe that new terms about language and style are unnecessary jargon, that unlike those in other fields such as psychology, economics, or chemistry, those of us concerned with mere writing ought to be able to make do with the good old terms learned in ninth-grade English. Those traditional terms won't suffice here, any more than traditional terms have sufficed in other lively fields of study. You will have to learn the meaning of a few new words like *nominalization, topic, thematic string,* and *resumptive modifier.* All told, there are fewer than a dozen new terms.

Some of these terms will be more familiar to those conversant with linguistic studies of the last quarter century. But even if you do recognize them, do not assume that we have kept their common meanings. We have had to rework both traditional and contemporary accounts of English specifically to make it possible to explain, not how sentences work within some system of grammatical theory, but the way contemporary readers work on sentences in the real world.

And finally, you should understand that this book is not an easy afternoon read. We offer detailed ways to put into specific practice the clichés of style: "Be clear," "Omit unnecessary words," "Devise a plan and stick to it." We suggest you read this book a short section at a time, then look at your own writing or the writing of others. If you think the writing is unclear in the ways we describe, revise it using the principle in question. If you think it is clear, revise it by reversing the principles and make the passage worse. Nothing highlights what counts as clear and direct better than seeing it in contrast with what is not. Under no circumstances try to devour this book in a sitting.

We readily acknowledge that not every writer will find our approach congenial. Many teachers and editors are certain that to write well, we must first read and absorb the style of the best prose writers. Then when writing, we first think through the problem at hand to understand our point clearly, then write sincerely, as if we were talking to a good friend about a serious subject. No doubt, many good writers have learned to write that way.

On the other hand, we have found that many other writers are comfortable with a more analytical account of writing, an approach that begins not with sincerity and good intentions, but with the principles behind the skilled construction of sentences and paragraphs, with the logic behind the thoughtful and deliberate ordering of ideas, with the ways one can use formal devices of style even to generate ideas—in short, an approach that concentrates not on the ambience of clear writing but on its craft. In no sense do we dismiss the importance of the writer's disposition toward the task. But we have worked with legions of writers who were thoughtful, sincere, well-intentioned, and very well-read, yet who could not write a clear, much less graceful, paragraph. We have also worked with legions of editors, teachers, and supervisors who have endlessly urged writers to be sincere, thoughtful, committed, etc., and have found that it did little good. Many have found in the approach that we offer here much that is useful and congenial. We also know that not every reader will.

Diagnostic Principles vs. Rigid Rules

Do not take what we offer here as draconian rules of composition, but rather as diagnostic principles of interpretation. We offer these principles as the basis for questions that allow a writer or editor to anticipate how readers are likely to respond to a piece of prose, a species of knowledge usually unavailable to writers when they unreflectively re-read their own writing. We are our own worst editors because we know too much about our subject to experience vicariously how a reader largely innocent of our knowledge will read. And to a reader-editor who must deal with the problems of someone else's writing, these questions will suggest ways to interpret the discomfort they often feel, to locate its source quickly, and to suggest ways to revise the prose that causes it.

Some teachers and writers resist principles of any kind as inimical to individual creativity. To them, the first six chapters in particular may seem to encourage stylistic homogeneity. Such a concern is, we believe, unfounded. The principles that characterize clear prose allow so many options within options that it is inconceivable we would find among the millions of writers in the

English-speaking world even a few who created sentences so alike that they would seem to have identical styles. These principles offer not prescriptions, but choices.

Prior Knowledge and Perceived Clarity

We also know that a particular passage of prose may seem not to reflect these principles, and yet to some readers will still seem entirely clear. That experience does not invalidate the principles we offer. The reason is this: What counts most in comprehending a text is how much we already know about its content. If we know a lot about viruses, we will be able to understand a badly written account of viruses better than someone who knows relatively little. We measure the quality of writing not just by what is objectively on a page, but by the way we feel as we construct new knowledge out of our experience with the words on the page. That feeling—good or bad—depends substantially on what we bring to that page.

The importance of prior knowledge suggests two points: First, since a competent writer usually knows his subject matter very well, perhaps too well, he is systematically handicapped in anticipating how easily readers will make sense of his text. Second, since a writer usually overestimates how much readers know, a writer should give readers more help than he thinks they need. This book lays out principles that help a writer predict how easily a reader will comprehend complex and unfamiliar material when that reader is not deeply versed in it. If the writer finds that his prose may hinder his intended reader, he can use these principles to suggest ways to revise it.

Some Intellectual Debts

The theory that lurks behind most of the views here is indebted to Noam Chomsky, Charles Fillmore, Jan Firbas, František Daneš, Nils Enkvist, Vic Yngve, among others. There are new debts. In Chapter 2, when I explicitly analogize the clearest style to narrative prose, I draw on some of the insights arising from recent work in two areas of cognitive psychology. One is schema theory, the other prototype semantics, particularly as developed by Eleanore Rosch.

The organization of each chapter reflects a familiar pedagogical principle supported by some recent work in educational psychology, a principle that most good teachers have long observed: When presenting complex new knowledge, first sketch a schematic structure that is too simple to reflect the complex reality of the subject; only then qualify, elaborate, and modify it. We have found that it is not effective to present new knowledge about language and style as a series of detailed, qualified, exception-laden observations. We may hope that out of that complexity students will construct a coherent whole faithful to the complex truth of things.

There are risks in both pedagogies. In the first way—a schematic structure that we then modify and qualify—we risk appearing to be superficial before we have a chance to qualify and elaborate. We also risk the possibility that the learner will learn only the simple structure and then caricature it. But the second way—teaching a structure of knowledge by simultaneously describing, qualifying, elaborating, complicating every detail— risks conceptual clutter. We assume that experience will modify and make more complex whatever simple structures we offer, but that experience only makes early confusion worse.

And Some Personal Debts

We must both acknowledge the help of colleagues who have regularly shared with us their insights about language and its complexities—Frank Kinahan, Don Freeman, George Gopen, Elizabeth Francis, Larry McEnerney. We must also thank the scores of graduate students who every year work to master these ideas and many others, in the blind faith that when it came time to teach them, it would all come together on opening night, as it always has. Several readers have generously offered their criticisms and suggestions. We, of course, are wholly responsible for what remains unclear.

By Gregory G. Colomb: Of my personal debts, the greatest is undoubtedly to my father, a man of business whose example helped me understand the truth in my favorite poet's maxim, that those "to whom Heav'n in Wit has been profuse," are obliged "to turn it to its use." Of course the largest burden fell on my family—

Sandra, BB, Karen, and the Beave, whose loving forebearance was too often tested but was always up to the mark.

By Joseph M. Williams: To my family—always amiably patient with my distractedness. Christopher, David, Joe, Megan, and Oliver—thanks for your love and good humor. And Joan, for your apparently bottomless well of patience and love.

The improvement of understanding is for two ends: first our own increase of knowledge; secondly to enable us to deliver that knowledge to others.

John Locke

Everything that can be thought at all can be thought clearly. Everything that can be said can be said clearly.

Ludwig Wittgenstein

Have something to say, and say it as clearly as you can. That is the only secret of style.

Matthew Arnold

The great enemy of clear language is insincerity . . .

George Orwell

In matters of grave importance, style, not sincerity, is the vital thing.

Oscar Wilde

1

Causes

Three Objectives

This is a book about writing clearly. I wish it could be short and simple like some others more widely known, but I want to do more than just urge writers to "Omit Needless Words" or "Be clear." Telling me to "Be clear" is like telling me to "Hit the ball squarely." I know that. What I don't know is how to do it. To explain how to write clearly, I have to go beyond platitudes.

But I want to do more than just help you write clearly. I also want you to understand this matter—to understand why some prose seems clear, other prose not, and why two readers might disagree about it; why a passive verb can be a better choice than an active verb; why so many truisms about style are either incomplete or wrong. More important, I want that understanding to consist not of anecdotal bits and pieces, but of a coherent system of principles more useful than "Write short sentences."

Now there is a lively debate about whether action and understanding have anything to do with each other, whether those who want to write clearly ought to study principles of language at all. You may write well, yet can't distinguish a subject from a verb, or you may understand everything from retained objects to the subjunctive pluperfect progressive, and still write badly. From this apparent contradiction many have concluded that we don't have to understand principles of grammar to write well. Writing well, they believe, has to do with being sincere, or writing how they speak, or finding their authentic voices, or just being born with the knack. Others devoutly believe that they learned to write well only because they studied Latin and diagrammed sentences beyond number.

The truth will disconcert those of both persuasions. Nostalgic anecdotes aside, the best evidence suggests that students who

1

spend a lot of time studying grammar improve their writing not one bit. In fact, they seem to get worse. On the other hand, there is good evidence that mature writers can change the way they write once they grasp a principled way of thinking about language, but one that is rather different from the kind of grammar some of us may dimly remember mastering—or being mastered by. The principles of style offered here will not describe sentences in a vocabulary that fifteenth-century students of Latin would still recognize, but in terms that help you understand how readers of modern English read; in terms that will help us understand why readers might describe the first sentence below as turgid and confusing, the second as clearer, more readable. But most important, in terms that also make it clear how to revise one into the other.

> 1a. The Committee proposal would provide for biogenetic industry certification of the safety to human health for new substances in requests for exemption from Federal rules.
>
> 1b. The Committee proposes that when the biogenetic industry requests the Agency to exempt new substances from Federal rules, the industry will certify that the substances are safe.

So if our first objective is doing, our second objective is understanding.

But however well a writer understands principles, it is not enough for those who also want to articulate that understanding to others, who want to explain why most readers prefer the style of (1b), and if necessary to persuade (or coerce) those others into writing in the same style. Whatever else a well-educated person can do, that person should be able to write clearly and to understand what it means to do that. But we judge as liberally educated the person who can articulate that understanding in ways that go beyond the ability to define subjects and verbs and explain their disagreements, certainly beyond self-evident truisms like "Be specific." This book provides a vocabulary that will let you explain these matters in ways that go beyond impressionism and banality.

A Very Short History of Bad Writing

Now, anyone familiar with the history of English prose might wonder whether anything we do here will substantially improve its future. Since the earliest times, many writers have graced us with much good writing. But others have afflicted us with much that is bad. Some of the reasons for the bad writing are rooted in history, others in personal experience.

In the last seven hundred years, English writers have responded to three influences on our language. Two are historical, one is cultural. These influences have helped make English a language flexible and precise enough to use with subjects ranging from the most concrete and mundane to the most abstract and elevated. But ironically, the very influences that have created this flexibility and precision have also allowed—indeed encouraged—many writers to produce prose that is quite bad. One of the two historical influences was the Norman Conquest in 1066, an event that led us to acquire a vocabulary qualitatively different from the Anglo-Saxon wordhord we've inherited from Bede, Alfred, and Aelfric. The second influence occurred in the sixteenth century, when Renaissance scholars struggling to translate Greek and Latin texts found themselves working at a lexical disadvantage.

After the Norman Conquest, those responsible for institutional, scholarly, and religious affairs wrote in Latin and later Norman French. In the late fourteenth and early fifteenth centuries, increasing numbers of writers began using English again for matters of state, commercial, and social life. But since the native vocabulary for these matters had long since disappeared (or had never come into being), English writers were able to write about them in the only vocabulary available, in words borrowed from Latin, but particularly from French. By the sixteenth century, French and Latin had disappeared from most institutional affairs, but writers were still using their words to refer to institutional concepts. As a result, the foundations were laid for a two-tiered vocabulary: one consisting of words common to daily life, the other of words having more special application.

Conspiring with that influence on our vocabulary was a second one, the Renaissance. In the sixteenth century, as England was increasingly influenced by classical writers, scholars began translating into English large numbers of Greek and Latin texts. But as one early writer put it "there ys many wordes in Latyn that we have no propre Englysh accordynge thereto," and so translators simply "Englished" foreign words, thereby providing us with another set of borrowings, many from Greek but most from Latin, and almost all of them more formal than either our native English vocabulary or the Anglicized words from French.

As a consequence of these two influences, our vocabulary is the most varied of any modern European language. Of the thousand words we use most frequently, over 80 percent descend from Anglo-Saxon. But most of them are the single syllable labor-intensive words: the articles *the, this, that, a,* etc.; most of the prepositions and pronouns: *in, on, of, by, at, with, you, we, it, I,* etc.; the most common verbs and most of the common nouns: *be, have, do, make, will, go, see, hand, head, mother, father, sun, man, woman,* etc. (Many words borrowed from French have lost any sense of formality: *people, (be)cause, use, just, really, very, sort, different, number, place.*)

When we refer to specific matters of our intellectual and artistic life, however, we use almost three times as many French and Latin content words as native English. Compare how I might have been obliged to write the paragraph before last, had on Hastings Field in 1066 a Norman arrow not mortally wounded Harold, the Anglo-Saxon King:

> Togetherworking with the outcome of the Norman Greatwin was the Newbirth. In the sixteenth yearhundred, as England was more shaped by the longread writers, the learned began turning into English many of the books of Athens and Rome, but as one early writer put it, "There ys many wordes in Latyn that we have no right Englysh withgoing thereto." So those who tongueturned works written in Latin and French into English only "Englished" outland words, thereby giving us yet more borrowed words, many from Greek but most from Latin, and almost all of them rather higher than the hereborn words or the words Englished from French.

Of course, if Harold had won the Battle of Hastings I wouldn't have written that at all, but he didn't, and as a result we now have a lexical resource that has endowed us with a stylistic flexibility largely unavailable to other modern languages. To express the precise shade of meaning and connotation, we can choose from among words borrowed from French—*bravery, mettle, valor, endurance, courage;* from Latin—*tenacity, fortitude,* and from words inherited from native English—*fearlessness, guts.*

But this flexibility has come with a price. Since the language of political, cultural, scientific, and economic affairs is based largely on Romance words, those of us who aspire to participate have had to learn a vocabulary separate from that which we learned through the first five or ten years of our lives. Just as we have to spend a good deal of time in school learning the idiosyncracies of our spelling system and of "good" grammar, so must we spend time learning words not rooted in our daily experience. Five-year-olds know the meaning of *between, over, across,* and *before,* but fifteen-year-olds have to learn the meaning of *intra-, supra-, trans-,* and *ante-.* To those of us already in an educated community, that vocabulary seems natural, not the least difficult. But if it were as natural to acquire as we think, publishers would not profit from selling books and tapes promising us Word Power in Thirty Days.

And of course once we learn these words, who among us can resist using them when we want to sound learned and authoritative? Writers began to surrender to that temptation well before the middle of the sixteenth century, but it was about then that many English writers became so enamored with an erudite vocabulary that they began deliberately to lard their prose with exotic Latinisms, a kind of writing that came to be known as the "inkhorn" style and was mocked as pretentious and incomprehensible by those critics for whom English had become a special passion. This impulse toward an elevated diction has proved quite durable; it accounts for the difference today between "The adolescents who had effectuated forcible entry into the domicile were apprehended" and "We caught the kids who broke into the house."

But while this Romance component of our vocabulary has contributed to one kind of stylistic inflation, it cannot alone account for a deeper problem we have with bad modern prose. We cannot point to the historical influence of borrowed words to explain why anyone would write (1a) rather than (1b) because (1b) has *more* borrowed words:

1a. The **Committee proposal** would **provide** for **biogenetic industry certification** of the **safety** to **human** health for new **substances** in **requests** for **exemption** from **Federal rules.**

1b. The **Committee proposes** that when the **biogenetic industry** requests the **Agency** to **exempt** new **substances** from **Federal rules,** the **industry** will **certify** that the **substances** are **safe.**

In addition to the influence of the Norman Conquest and the Renaissance, there has been another, more subtle historical influence on our prose style, an influence that some linguists have speculated to be a kind of stylistic destiny for literate societies. As societies become intellectually mature, it has been claimed, their writers seem increasingly to replace specific verbs with abstract nouns. It allegedly happened in Sanskrit prose, in the prose of many Western European languages, and it seems to be happening in modern English. What centrally distinguishes sentence (1a) from (1b) is not the historical source of their vocabulary, but the abstract nouns in (1a) in contrast to the shorter and more specific verbs and adjective of (1b):

1a. The Committee **proposal** would provide for biogenetic industry **certification** of the **safety** to human health for new substances requested for **exemption** from Federal rules.

1b. The Committee **proposes** that when the biogenetic industry **requests** the Agency to **exempt** new substances from Federal rules, the industry will **certify** that the substances are **safe**.

These nouns alone make a style more abstract, but they encourage more abstraction: once a writer expresses actions in nouns, she can then eliminate whatever (usually concrete) agents perform those actions along with those whom the actions affect:

The proposal would provide for certification of the safety of new substances in requests for exemption.

These abstract Romance nouns result in a prose that we variously call gummy, turgid, obtuse, prolix, complex, or unreadable. An early example:

If use and custom, having the help of so long time and continuance wherein to [re]fine our tongue, of so great learning and experience which furnish matter for the [re]fining, of so good wits and judgments which can tell how to [re]fine, have griped at nothing in all that time, with all that cunning, by all those wits which they will not let go but hold for most certain in the right of our writing, that then our tongue ha[s] no certainty to trust to, but write all at random. But the antecedent, in my opinion, is altogether unpossible, wherefore the consequent is a great deal more th[a]n probable, which is that our tongue ha[s] in her own possession and writing very good evidence to prove her own right writing; which, though no man as yet by any public writing of his seem[s] to have seen, yet the tongue itself is ready to show them to any whosoever

which is able to read them and withal to judge what evidence is right in the right of writing.
—Richard Mulcaster, *The First Part of the Elementary*, 1582

Other sixteenth-century writers were able to write prose not wholly free of abstraction, but not burdened by it either, a prose that we would judge today to be clear, direct, and still readable (I have changed only the spelling and punctuation):

> Among all other lessons this should first be learned, that we never affect any strange inkhorn terms, but to speak as is commonly received, neither seeking to be over-fine, nor yet living overcareless, suiting our speech as most men do, and ordering our wits as the fewest have done. Some seek so far for outlandish English that they forget altogether their mother's language. And I dare swear this, if some of their mothers were alive, they [would] not [be] able to tell what they say. And yet these fine English clerks will say they speak in their mother tongue, if a man should charge them for counterfeiting the King's English.
> —Thomas Wilson, *Art of Rhetoric*, 1553

By the middle of the seventeenth century, this impulse toward "over-fine" prose had infected scholarly writing. Shortly after the Royal Society was established in 1660, Thomas Spratt, one of its historians, complained that scientific writing suffered from a "vicious abundance of phrase, [a] trick of metaphors, [a] volubility of tongue which makes so great a noise in the world." Better, he said, to

> reject all the amplifications, digressions, and swellings of style: to return back to the primitive purity, and shortness, when men deliver'd so many things, almost in an equal number of words . . . [to prefer] the language of Artizans, Countrymen, and Merchants, before that, of Wits, or Scholars.
> —From *The History of the Royal Society*

When the New World was settled, American writers had a chance to create such a prose style, one lean and sinewy fit for a new society. But we did not. Early in the nineteenth century, James Fenimore Cooper complained that "the common faults of American language are an ambition of effect, a want of simplicity, and a turgid abuse of terms":

> The love of turgid expressions is gaining ground, and ought to be corrected. One of the most certain evidences of a man of high

breeding, is his simplicity of speech: a simplicity that is equally removed from vulgarity and exaggeration. . . . He does not say, in speaking of a dance, that "the attire of the ladies was exceedingly elegant and peculiarly becoming at the late assembly," but that "the women were well dressed at the last ball"; nor is he apt to remark, "that the Rev. Mr G—— gave us an elegant and searching discourse the past sabbath," but that "the parson preached a good sermon last sunday."

The utterance of a gentleman ought to be deliberate and clear, without being measured. . . . Simplicity should be the firm aim, after one is removed from vulgarity, and let the finer shades of accomplishment be acquired as they can be attained. In no case, however, can one who aims at turgid language, exaggerated sentiments, or pedantic utterances, lay claim to be either a man or a woman of the world.

—James Fenimore Cooper, *The American Democrat*, 1838

In these sentiments, Cooper reflects a long tradition about what constitutes genteel behavior in the English-speaking world. For five hundred years, writers on courtesy have urged aspiring gentle people to avoid speech that is loquacious, flamboyant, or pompous, to keep their language plain, modest, and unassuming. In *The American Democrat*, Cooper was attempting to define what constituted an American gentleman in a democratic world.

But in Cooper's own style we can see the inexorable power of that ambition of effect, want of simplicity, and turgid abuse of terms, for he demonstrated—unconsciously, it would seem—the very style he condemned. Had he been aware of his own language, he would have avoided those abstract, mostly Romance nouns—*love, expressions, simplicity, speech, vulgarity, exaggeration, utterance, simplicity, aim, accomplishment, claim* for something closer to this:

We should discourage writers who love turgid language. A well-bred man speaks simply, in a way that is neither vulgar nor exaggerated. . . . He does not say of a dance that "the attire of the ladies was exceedingly elegant and peculiarly becoming at the late assembly," but that "the women were well-dressed at the last ball"; nor does he remark that "the Rev. Mr G—— gave us an elegant and searching discourse the past Sabbath," but that "the parson preached a good sermon last Sunday."

A gentleman does not measure his words, but speaks them deliberately and clearly. After he rids [his language] of vulgarity, he should aim at simplicity, and then, as he can, acquire the finer shades of accomplishment. No one can claim to be a man or woman of the world who deliberately speaks in turgid or pedantic language or who exaggerates sentiments.

In fact, after abusing the pretentious style of "The attire of the ladies was elegant," he echoed it in his own next sentence: "The utterance of a gentleman ought to be deliberate. . . ."

About a half century later, Mark Twain demonstrated the style that we now like to identify as American—clear, straight, and plainspoken:

> There have been daring people in the world who claimed that Cooper could write English, but they are all dead now—all dead but Lounsbury [a scholar who praised Cooper's novels]. I don't remember that Lounsbury makes the claim in so many words, still he makes it, for he says that *Deerslayer* is a "pure work of art." Pure, in that connection, means faultless—faultless in all details—and language is a detail. If Mr. Lounsbury writes himself—but it is plain that he didn't; and so it is likely that he imagines until this day that Cooper's [style] is as clean and compact as his own. Now I feel sure, deep down in my heart, that Cooper wrote about the poorest English that exists in our language.[3]

Unfortunately, twentieth-century writers have not all followed Twain's example.

In probably the best-known essay on English style in the twentieth century, "Politics and the English Language," George Orwell described turgid language when it is used by politicians, bureaucrats, and other chronic dodgers of responsibility. Orwell's advice is sound enough:

> The keynote [of such a style] is the elimination of simple verbs. Instead of being a single word, such as *break, stop, spoil, mend, kill,* a verb becomes a *phrase,* made up of a noun or adjective tacked on to some general-purposes verb such as *prove, serve, form, play, render.* In addition, the passive voice is wherever possible used in preference to the active, and noun constructions are used instead of gerunds (*by examination* of instead of *by examining*). The range of verbs is further cut down by means of the *-ize* and *de*-formations, and the banal statements are given an appearance of profundity by means of the *not un*-formation.

But in the very act of anatomizing the turgid style, Orwell demonstrated it in his own. Had Orwell himself avoided making a verb a phrase, had he avoided the passive voice, had he avoided noun constructions, he would have written something closer to this (I begin with a phrase Orwell used a few lines earlier):

> When writers dodge the work of constructing prose, they eliminate simple verbs. Instead of using a single word, such as *break, stop, spoil, mend, kill,* they turn the verb into a phrase made up of a noun or adjective; then they tack it on to some general-purposes verb such as *prove, serve, form, play, render.* Wherever possible, such writers use the passive voice instead of the active and noun constructions instead of gerunds (*by examination* instead of *by examining*). They cut down the range of verbs further when they use *-ize* and *de-*formations and try to make banal statements seem profound by the *not un-*formation.

If Orwell could not avoid this kind of passive, abstract style in his own writing (and I don't believe that he was trying to be ironic), we ought not be surprised that the prose style of our academic, scholarly, and professional writers is often worse. On the language of social scientists:

> a turgid and polysyllabic prose does seem to prevail in the social sciences. . . . Such a lack of ready intelligibility, I believe, usually has little or nothing to do with the complexity of thought. It has to do almost entirely with certain confusions of the academic writer about his own status.
> —C. Wright Mills, *The Sociological Imagination*

On the language of medicine:

> It now appears that obligatory obfuscation is a firm tradition within the medical profession. . . . [Medical writing] is a highly skilled, calculated attempt to confuse the reader. . . . A doctor feels he might get passed over for an assistant professorship because he wrote his papers too clearly—because he made his ideas seem too simple.
> —Michael Crichton, *New England Journal of Medicine*

On the language of the law:

> in law journals, in speeches, in classrooms and in courtrooms, lawyers and judges are beginning to worry about how often they have been misunderstood, and they are discovering that sometimes they cannot even understand each other.
> —Tom Goldstein, *New York Times*

In short, bad writing has been with us for a long time, and its roots run wide in our culture and deep into its history.

Some Private Causes of Bad Writing

These historical influences alone would challenge those of us who want to write well, but many of us also have to deal with problems of a more personal sort. Michael Crichton cited one: some of us feel compelled to use pretentious language to make ideas that we think are too simple seem more impressive. In the same way, others use difficult and therefore intimidating language to protect what they have from those who want a share of it: the power, prestige, and privilege that go with being part of the ruling class. We can keep knowledge from those who would use it by locking it up, but we can also hide facts and ideas behind language so impenetrable that only those trained in its use can find them.

Another reason some of us may write badly is that we are seized by the memory of an English teacher for whom the only kind of good writing was writing free of errors which only that teacher understood: fused genitives, dangling participles, split infinitives. For many such writers, filling a blank page is now like laying a minefield; they are concerned less with clarity and precision than with survival.

Finally, some of us write badly not because we intend to or because we never learned how, but because occasionally we seem to experience transient episodes of stylistic aphasia. Occasionally, many of us write substantially less well than we know we can, but we seem unable to do anything about it. This kind of dismaying regression typically occurs when we are writing about matters that we do not entirely understand, for readers who do. This problem afflicts most severely those who are just getting started in a new field of knowledge, typically students who are learning how to think and write in some academic area or profession new to them, in some well-defined "community of discourse" to which they do not yet belong.

All such communities have a body of knowledge that their apprentices must acquire, characteristic ways of thinking about problems, of making and evaluating arguments. And just as important, each community articulates its arguments in a characteristic voice: lawyers talk and write in ways distinct from physicians, whose style is distinct from sociologists, whose style is distinct from philosophers. When a writer new to a field is simultaneously trying to master its new knowledge, its new style of thinking, and its new voice, she is unlikely to manage all those new competencies equally well. Some aspect of her performance will deteriorate: typically the quality of her writing.

I once discussed these matters at a seminar on legal writing. At the end, a woman volunteered that I had recounted her academic history. She had earned a Ph.D. in anthropology, published several books and articles, and been judged a good writer. But she became bored with anthropology and went to law school, where during the first few months she thought she was developing a degenerative brain disorder: she could no longer write clear, concise English prose. She was experiencing a breakdown like that experienced by many students taking an introductory course in a complex field—a period of cognitive overload, a condition that predictably degrades their powers of written expression.

Here is a passage from the first paper written by a first year law student who as an undergraduate had been evaluated as a superior writer.

> The final step in Lord Morris's preparation to introduce the precedents is his consideration of the idea of conviction despite the presence of duress and then immediate pardon for that crime as an unnecessary step which is in fact injurious for it creates the stigma of the criminal on a potentially blameless (or at least not criminal) individual.

This means,

> Before Lord Morris introduces the precedents, he considers a final issue: If a court convicts a defendant who acted under duress and then immediately pardons that defendant, the court may have taken an unnecessary step, a step that may even injure the defendant, if it stigmatizes him as criminal when he may be blameless.

This writer had to juggle several related actions, few of which he entirely understood, much less how they were related. When he had to express his confused ideas, he dumped onto the page all the concepts that seemed relevant, expressing them in abstractions loosely tied together with all-purpose prepositions.

Now here is a great irony: As he struggles with his ideas, his prose predictably degenerates. But much of what he is reading for the first time (and is probably also trying to imitate) typically suffers from the same clotted abstraction:

Because the individualized assessment of the appropriateness of the death penalty is a moral inquiry into the culpability of the defendant, and not an emotional response to the mitigating evidence, I agree with the Court that an instruction informing the jury that they "must not be swayed by mere sentiment, conjecture, sympathy, passion, prejudice, public opinion or public feeling" does not by itself violate the Eighth and Fourteenth Amendments to the United States Constitution.
—Sandra Day O'Connor, concurring, *California v. Albert Greenwood Brown, Jr.*, no. 85-1563)

This means,

When a jury assesses whether the death penalty is appropriate in individual cases, it must not respond to mitigating evidence emotionally but rather inquire into the defendant's moral culpability. I therefore agree with the majority: When a court informs a jury that it "must not be swayed by mere sentiment, conjecture, sympathy, passion, prejudice, public opinion or public feeling," the court has not violated the defendant's rights under the Eighth and Fourteenth Amendments.

In other words, as a novice in a field reads its professional prose, he will predictably try to imitate those features of style that seem most prominently to bespeak membership, professional authority. And in complex professional prose, no feature of style is more typical than clumps of Latinate abstractions:

individualized **assessment** of the **appropriateness** of the death **penalty** . . . a moral **inquiry** into the **culpability** of the defendant.

Simultaneously, if a writer new to a field does not entirely control his ideas, his own prose will often slip into a style characterized by those same clumps of abstraction:

consideration of the idea of **conviction** despite the **presence** of **duress** and then immediate **pardon**.

What we should find astonishing is not that so many young writers write badly, but that any of them writes well.

It may be that in these circumstances most of us have to pass through some dark valley of stylistic infelicity. But once we realize that we are experiencing a common anguish, we may be less dismayed by our failures, or at least those failures will seem explicable. If we understand some of the specific ways that our prose is likely to break down, and are able to articulate to ourselves and to others the reasons and the ways, we might even be able to do something about it.

As I write these sentences, though, hovering over my shoulder is another critic of English style. About fifty years ago H. L. Mencken wrote,

> With precious few exceptions, all the books on style in English are by writers quite unable to write. The subject, indeed, seems to exercise a special and dreadful fascination over school ma'ams, bucolic college professors, and other such pseudoliterates. . . . Their central aim, of course, is to reduce the whole thing to a series of simple rules—the overmastering passion of their melancholy order, at all times and everywhere.

Mencken is right, of course: no one can teach clear writing by rule or principle, simple or not, to those who have nothing to say and no reason to say it, to those who cannot think or feel or see. But I also know that many who see well and think carefully and feel deeply still cannot write clearly. I also know that learning to write clearly can help us think and feel and see, and that in fact there are a few straightforward principles—not rules—that help.

Here they are.

Suit the action to the word, the word to the action.
William Shakespeare

Action is eloquence.
William Shakespeare

Words and deeds are quite different modes of the divine energy.
Words are also actions, and actions are a kind of words.
Ralph Waldo Emerson

I am not built for academic writings. Action is my domain.
Gandhi

2

Clarity

Finding a Useful Language: Some First Steps

How might we describe the difference between these two sentences?

1a. Because we knew nothing about local conditions, we could not determine how effectively the committee had allocated funds to areas that most needed assistance.

1b. Our lack of knowledge about local conditions precluded determination of committee action effectiveness in fund allocation to those areas in greatest need of assistance.

Most of us would call the style of (1a) clearer, more concise than the style of (1b). We would probably call (1b) turgid, indirect, unclear, unreadable, passive, confusing, abstract, awkward, opaque, complex, impersonal, wordy, prolix, obscure, inflated. But when we use *clear* for one and *turgid* for the other, we do not describe sentences on the page; we describe how we feel about them. Neither *awkward* nor *turgid* are on the page. Turgid and awkward refer to a bad feeling behind my eyes.

To account for style in a way that lets us go beyond saying how we feel, we need a way to explain how we get those impressions. Some would have us count syllables and words—the fewer the better, according to most such schemes. But if we counted every syllable and word we wrote, we would spend more time counting than writing. More to the point, numbers don't explain what makes a sentence awkward or turgid, much less tell anyone how to turn it into a clear and graceful one. And even if counting did tell us when a passage was hard to read, we shouldn't have to count if we knew that it was hard to read just by reading it.

The words we use to communicate our impressions cannot alone constitute a vocabulary sufficient to describe style, but they

are part of one, and so before we move on to a new way of thinking and talking about style, we should reflect on how we use
those words. Here are three more sentences that we could say are
in some sense "unclear," which is to say, sentences that make us
feel we have to work harder than we think we ought to (or want
to). But do they seem "unclear" in the same way?

2. Decisions in regard to the administration of medication despite
   the inability of irrational patients voluntarily appearing in
   Trauma Centers to provide legal consent rest with a physician
   alone.

3. China, so that it could expand and widen its influence and importance among the Eastern European nations, in 1955 began
   in a quietly orchestrated way a diplomatic offensive directed
   against the Soviet Union.

4. When pAD4038 in the *E. coli pmiimanA* mutant CD1 hetero-
   logously overexpressed the *P. aeruginosa pmi* gene, there
   appeared high levels of PMI and GMP activities that were de-
   tectable only when pAD4038 was present.

Sentence (2) makes us work too hard because we have to sort
out and then mentally re-assemble several actions expressed
mostly as abstract nouns—*decisions, administration, medication, inability, consent*—actions that are also arranged in a way
that both distorts their underlying sequence and obscures who
performs them. When we revise the abstract nouns into verbs expressing actions, when we make their actors the subjects of those
verbs and rearrange the events into a chronological sequence, we
create a sentence that we could call "clear" because as we read it,
it does not confuse us:

2a. When a patient voluntarily appears at a Trauma Center but
    behaves so irrationally that he cannot legally consent to treat-
    ment, only a physician can decide whether to administer
    medication.*

---

*Many readers would revise the original passages more radically than I have.
And they would be right to do so. But if I completely rewrote these sentences, I
would show only that I was able to rethink the whole idea of the sentence, usually
a good thing but not something that can be easily taught. Principled revision
would remain a mystery. So for pedagogical reasons, I stay close to the content of
each original sentence to demonstrate that we can improve murky sentences
without relying on a talent that comes only through experience.

Sentence (3) seems less than entirely clear and direct not because the writer used too many abstract nouns, displaced its actors, and confused the sequence of events, but because he separated parts of the sentence that he should have kept together and because he used more words than he needed. Here's (3) revised:

> 3a. In 1955, China began to orchestrate a quiet diplomatic offensive against the Soviet Union to expand its influence in Eastern Europe.

Sentence (4) seems unclear not because the writer fell into abstractions or split elements of the sentence, but because she used words that most of us do not understand. If that sentence baffles us, it is clear to someone who knows the field.

The single impressionistic word "unclear" can mask a variety of problems. To correct those problems, we need not avoid impressionistic language; but we do have to use it precisely, and then move beyond it. If we sharpen our impressionistic language a bit, we might say that sentence (2) feels unclear because it is "abstract" or "turgid"; (3) is unclear because it is "disjointed," or does not "flow." If sentence (4) seems incomprehensible, it is because we don't understand the technical language; it is "too technical."

It is at this point that we need that second vocabulary, one that will help us explain what it is that makes us want to call a passage turgid or disjointed, a vocabulary that also suggests how we can revise it. In this chapter, we're going to discuss the particular kind of unclarity that we feel in (1b) and (2), the kind of sentences that feel gummy, lumpy, abstract; the kind of sentences that—depending on their subject matter—we variously characterize as academese, legalese, medicalese, bureaucratese. In the following chapters, we'll discuss different kinds of unclear writing.

Telling Stories

Stories are among the first kinds of continuous discourse we learn. From the time we are children, we all tell stories to achieve a multitude of ends—to amuse, to warn, to excite, to inform, to explain, to persuade. Storytelling is fundamental to human behavior. No other form of prose can communicate large amounts of information so quickly and persuasively. At first glance, most academic and professional writing seems to consist not of narrative but of explanation. But even prose that may seem wholly discursive and abstract usually has behind it the two central components of a story—characters and their actions. There are no characters visible in (5a), but that doesn't mean there aren't any; compare (5b):

5a. The current estimate is of a 50% reduction in the introduction of new chemical products in the event that compliance with the Preliminary Manufacturing Notice becomes a requirement under proposed Federal legislation.

5b. If **Congress** requires that **the chemical industry** comply with the Preliminary Manufacturing Notice, **we** estimate that **the industry** will introduce 50% fewer new products.

It may even be a story whose main characters are concepts:

Because the intellectual foundations of evolution are the same as so many other scientific theories, the falsification of their foundations would be necessary for the replacement of evolutionary theory with creationism.

We can make theories play the roles of competing characters:

In contrast to **creationism, the theory of evolution** shares its intellectual foundations with **many other theories.** As a result, **creationism** will displace **evolutionary theory** only when **it** can first prove that the foundations of **all those other theories** are false.

We can see how pairs of sentences like these tell the "same" story in different ways if we start with a story that seems clear and then change the way it represents characters and their actions:

Though the Governor knew that the cities needed new revenues to improve schools, he vetoed the budget bill because he wanted to encourage cities to increase local taxes.

What's the story here, which is to say, who are the characters and what are they doing? The characters are the Governor, the cities, and the schools (the legislature is also in there, but hidden). The Governor is part of three actions: he *knew* something, he *vetoed* a bill, and he *will encourage* the cities; the cities are part of three actions: they *need* revenues, they [should] *improve* schools, and they [should] *increase* taxes; and the schools are part of one action: they will be *improved*. Those six actions are all represented by the same part of speech—they are all verbs. And that part of speech—the verb—is singularly important to why we think that this sentence about the Governor and the schools is reasonably clear.

Before you read on, rewrite that story, but instead of using those six verbs to express actions, use their noun forms. Three of the noun forms are different from the verbs: *to know* → *knowledge, to encourage* → *encouragement, to improve* → *improvement*. The other three nouns are identical to their corresponding verbs: *to need* → *the need, to veto* → *the veto, to increase* → *the increase*.

Here is a version using nouns instead of verbs. Yours may differ.

> Despite his **knowledge** of the **need** by cities for new revenues for the **improvement** of their schools, the Governor executed a **veto** of the budget bill to give **encouragement** to the cities for an **increase** of local taxes.

At some level of meaning, this sentence offers the same story as the original. But at another level—at the level of how readers perceive voice, style, clarity, ease of understanding—it is different; for most of us, I hope, worse.

It is in this difference between the ways we can tell the "same" story that we locate the first principles of clear writing (which is to say, you will recall, writing that makes the reader feel clear about what he is reading).

The First Two Principles of Clear Writing

Readers are likely to feel that they are reading prose that is clear and direct when

(1) the subjects of the sentences name the cast of characters, and

(2) the verbs that go with those subjects name the crucial actions those characters are part of.

Look again at (1b):

1b. Our lack of knowledge about local conditions precluded determination of committee action effectiveness in fund allocation to those areas in greatest need of assistance.

Who are the characters? If we were to cast this sentence as a play, how many parts would we have to fill? There is "we" (in the form of *our*); there is "the committee" (are they also "we?"); and there are "areas." But where in (1b) do those characters appear? *Our* is not a subject, but a modifier of *lack:* our lack. *Committee* is not a subject, but another modifier: committee action effectiveness. And *areas* is not a subject either, but the object of a preposition: to areas. What is the subject of (1b)? An abstraction: *Our lack of knowledge,* followed by its vague verb *precluded.*

Now look at (1a):

1a. Because we knew nothing about local conditions, we could not determine how effectively the committee had allocated funds to areas that most needed assistance.

We is the subject of both *knew* and *could not determine:*

Because we knew nothing . . . , we could not determine. . . .

The committee is subject of the verb *had allocated:*

the committee had allocated.

And although *area* is still the object of a preposition (*to areas*), it is also the subject of *needed:*

areas that most needed assistance.

Sentence (1b) consistently violates the first principle: use subjects to name characters; sentence (1a) consistently observes it.

Consider how those two sentences name the actions those characters perform. In the first, the actions are not verbs, but rather abstract nouns: *lack, knowledge, determination, action, allocation, assistance, need.* The second consistently names those actions in verbs: *we knew nothing, we could not determine, the committee allocated, areas needed.* The only action still a noun is *assistance.* So the first sentence violates not only our first principle: name characters in subjects; it violates the second as well: express crucial actions in verbs. And again, the second sentence observes both principles. The real difference between those sentences, then, lies not in their numbers of syllables or words, but in where the writer placed the characters and expressed their actions.

The principle also gives us some simple advice about revising: When your prose feels turgid, abstract, too complex, do two things. First, locate the cast of characters and the actions that those characters perform (or are the objects of). If you find that those characters are not subjects and their actions are not verbs, revise so that they are.

But even when we don't feel anything wrong with our own prose, others often do, so we ought to do something that will let us anticipate that judgment. A quick method is simply to run a line under the first five or six words of every sentence. If you find that (1) you have to go more than six or seven words into a sentence to get past the subject to the verb and (2) the subject of the sentence is not one of your characters, take a hard look at that sentence; its characters and actions probably do not align with subjects and verbs. (If you want to do a more exact and thorough analysis, underline the subject of every verb, even those in subordinate clauses.) Then simply revise the sentence so that characters appear as subjects and their actions as verbs.

In some cases, we exclude characters altogether. If we had the context of this next passage, we might know who was doing what:

> The argument that failure to provide for preservation of the royalty rate upon expiration of the patent discouraged challenges to the contract does not apply here.

Presumably, the writer knew who was arguing, failing, challenging—though often those who write like this in fact do not know. If we invent characters as if we knew who they were and make them subjects and their actions verbs, we can revise this sentence as we have others:

> **Harris** *argues* that when **Smith** *gave* him no way to *preserve* the royalty rate when **the patent** *expired,* **Smith** *discouraged* him from challenging their contract. But **that argument** *does* not *apply* here.

Some readers may think that I am simply giving the standard advice about avoiding passive verbs. As we'll see in a few pages, that's not bad advice, but nothing we have seen so far has anything directly to do with passive verbs. In fact, not one of the "bad" examples in this chapter so far has in it a single passive verb. The bad examples "feel" passive, but that feeling does not arise from passive verbs but rather from abstract nouns and missing characters.

Some Stylistic Consequences

We begin with these two principles—characters as subjects and their actions as verbs—because they have so many unexpected but welcome consequences:

• You may have been told to write more specifically, more concretely.

When we turn verbs into nouns and then delete the characters, we fill a sentence with abstraction:

> There has been an affirmative **decision** for program **termination.**

When we use subjects to name characters and verbs to name their actions, we write sentences that are specific and concrete.

> *The Director* **decided** to **terminate** the program.

• You may have been told to avoid using too many prepositional phrases.

> An evaluation **of** the program **by** us will allow greater efficiency **in** service **to** clients.

While it is not clear what counts as "too many," it is clear that when we use verbs instead of abstract nouns, we can also eliminate most of the prepositional phrases. Compare,

> We will evaluate the program so that we can serve clients better.

• You may have been told to put your ideas in a logical order.

When we turn verbs into nouns and then string them through prepositional phrases, we can confuse the logical sequence of the actions. This series of actions distorts the "real" chronological sequence:

> The **closure** of the branch and the **transfer** of its business and non-unionized employees **constituted** an unfair labor practice because the purpose of **obtaining** an economic benefit by means of **discouraging** unionization motivated the **closure** and **transfer.**

When we use subjects to name characters and verbs to name their actions, we are more likely to match our syntax to the logic of our story:

> The partners **committed** an unfair labor practice when they **closed** the branch and **transferred** its business and nonunionized em-

ployees in order to **discourage** unionization and thereby **obtain** an economic benefit.

• You may have been told to use connectors to clarify logical relationships:

> The more effective presentation of needs by other Agencies resulted in our failure in acquiring federal funds, despite intensive lobbying efforts on our part.

When you turn nouns into verbs, you have to use logical operators like *because, although,* and *if* to link the new sequences of clauses.

> **Although** we lobbied Congress intensively, we could not acquire federal funds **because** other interests presented their needs more effectively.

• You may have been told to write short sentences.

In fact, there is nothing wrong with a long sentence if its subjects and verbs match its characters and actions. But even so, when we match subjects and verbs with characters and actions, we almost always write a shorter sentence. Compare the original and revised sentences we've looked at so far.

In short, when you observe this first pair of principles, you reap other benefits. Once you grasp the two root principles, you can apply them quickly, knowing that as you correct one problem, you are solving others. When you align subjects and characters, verbs and actions, you turn abstract, impersonal, apparently expository prose into a form that feels much more like a narrative, into something closer to a story.

I should clarify an often misunderstood point: clear writing does not require Dick-and-Jane sentences. Almost all of the revisions are shorter than the originals, but the objective is not curtness: what counts is not the number of words in a sentence, but how easily we get from beginning to end while understanding everything in between. This was written by an undergraduate attempting academic sophistication:

> After Czar Alexander II's emancipation of the Russian serfs in 1861, many now-free peasants chose to live on a commune for purposes of cooperation in agricultural production as well as for social stability. Despite some communes' attempts at economic and social equalization through the strategy of imposing a low

economic status on the peasants, which resulted in their reduction to near-poverty, a centuries-long history of important social distinctions even among serfs prevented social equalization.

In his struggle to follow the principles we've covered here, he revised that paragraph into a primer style:

> In 1861, Czar Alexander II emancipated the Russian serfs. Many of them chose to live on agricultural communes. There they thought they could cooperate with one another in agricultural production. They could also create a stable social structure. The leaders of some of these communes tried to equalize the peasants economically and socially. As one strategy, they tried to impose on all a low economic status that reduced them to near-poverty. However, the communes failed to equalize them socially because even serfs had made important social distinctions among themselves for centuries.

In Chapter 7 we discuss some ways to manage long sentences. As we'll see there, some of those same techniques suggest ways to change a series of too-short, too-simple sentences into a style that is more complex, more mature, but still readable. Applying those principles, the student revised once more:

> After the Russian serfs were emancipated by Czar Alexander II in 1861, many chose to live on agricultural communes, hoping they could cooperate in working the land and establish a stable social structure. At first, those who led some of the communes tried to equalize the new peasants socially and economically by imposing on them all a low economic status, a strategy that reduced them to near-poverty. But the communes failed to equalize them socially because for centuries the serfs had observed among themselves important social distinctions.

As we might expect, the principles of aligning characters with subjects and actions with verbs have exceptions. We will see later how we must choose *which* character from among many to make the subject and *which* action to make the verb. At this point, though, we can represent our two principles simply and graphically:

FIXED	SUBJECT	VERB	COMPLEMENT
VARIABLE	CHARACTERS	ACTION	———

As we read a sentence, we have to integrate two levels of its structure: one is its predictable grammatical sequence: Subject + Verb + Complement; the other level is its story, a level of meaning whose parts have no fixed order: Characters + Actions. To a significant degree, we judge a style to be clear or unclear according to how consistently a writer aligns those two levels. We usually feel we are reading prose that is clear, direct, and readable when a writer consistently expresses the crucial actions of her story in verbs and her central characters (real or abstract) in their subjects. We usually feel that we are reading prose that is gummy, abstract, and difficult when a writer unnecessarily dislocates actions from verbs and (almost by necessity) locates her characters away from subjects, or deletes them entirely. There are details about these principles worth examining.

Subjects and Characters

There are many kinds of characters. The most important are agents, the direct source of an action or condition. There are collective agents:

Faculties of national eminence do not always teach well.

secondary or remote agents:

Mayor Daley built Chicago into a giant among cities.

and even figurative agents that stand for the real agents:

The White House announced today the President's schedule.

The business sector is cooperating.

Many instances of malignant tumors fail to seek attention.

In some sentences, we use subjects to name things that are really the means, the instrument by which some unstated agent performs an action, making the instrument seem like the agent of that action.

Studies of coal production reveal these figures.

These new data establish the need for more detailed analysis.

This evidence proves my theory.

That is,

When **we study** coal production, **we find** these figures.

> I have established through these new data that we must analyze the problem in more detail.

> With this evidence I prove my theory.

In the original sentences, the instruments act so much like agents that there is little point in revising them.

Some characters do not appear in a sentence at all, so that when we revise, we have to supply them:

> In the last sentence of the Gettysburg Address there is a rallying cry for the continuation of the struggle.

> In the last sentence of the Gettysburg Address, Lincoln rallied his audience to continue the struggle against the South.

In other sentences, the writer may imply a character in an adjective:

> Determination of policy occurs at the presidential level.

> The President determines policy.

> Medieval theological debates often addressed what to modern thought seems to be metaphysical triviality.

> Medieval theologians often debated issues that we might think were metaphysically trivial.

And in some cases, the characters and their actions are so far removed from the surface of a sentence that if we want to be explicit, we have to recast the sentence entirely.

> There seems to be no obvious reason that would account for the apparent unavailability of evidence relevant to the failure of this problem to yield to standard solutions.

> I do not know why my staff cannot find evidence to explain why we haven't been able to solve this problem in the ways we have before.

Most often, though, characters in abstract prose modify one of those abstract nouns or are objects of prepositions such as *by, of, on the part of*:

> The Federalists' belief that the instability *of* government was a consequence *of* popular democracy was based on their belief in the tendency *on the part of* factions to further their self-interest at the expense of the common good.

The Federalists believed that **popular democracy** destabilized **government** because **they** believed that **factions** tended to further their self-interest at the expense of the common good.

Often, we have to supply indefinite subjects, because the sentence expresses a general statement:

Such multivariate strategies may be of more use in understanding the genetic factors which contribute to vulnerability to psychiatric disorders than strategies based on the assumption that the presence or absence of psychopathology is dependent on a major gene or than strategies in which a single biological variable is studied.

If **we/one/researchers** are to understand the genetic factors that make some patients vulnerable to psychiatric disorders, **we/one/researchers** should use multivariate strategies rather than strategies in which **we/one/researchers** study only a single biological variable.

As flexible as English is, it does have a problem with indefinite subjects. Unlike writers of French, who have available an impersonal pronoun that does not seem excessively formal, English has no convenient indefinite pronoun. In this book, we have used *we* quite freely, because parts of this book are written by two people. But many readers dislike the royal *we* when used by a single writer, because they think it pretentious. Even when used by two or more writers, it can be misleading because it includes too many referents: the writer, the reader, and an indefinite number of others. As a consequence, many writers slip back into nominalizations or, as we shall see in a bit, passive verbs:

If the generic factors that make some patients vulnerable to psychiatric disorders **are to be understood,** multivariate strategies **should be used** rather than strategies in which **it is assumed** that a major gene causes psychopathology or strategies in which only a single biological variable **is studied.**

Verbs and Actions

As we'll use the word here, "action" will cover not only physical movement, but also mental processes, feelings, relationships, literal or figurative. In these next four sentences, the meaning becomes clearer as the verbs become more specific:

There **has been** effective staff information dissemination control on the part of the Secretary.

The Secretary **has exercised** effective staff information dissemination control.

The Secretary **has** effectively **controlled** staff information dissemination.

The Secretary **has** effectively **controlled** how his staff **disseminates** information.

The crucial actions aren't *be* or *exercise,* but *control* and *disseminate.*

Most writers of turgid prose typically use a verb not to express action but merely to state that an action exists.

A *need* **exists** for greater candidate *selection* **efficiency.**	=	We *must* **select** candidates more efficiently.
There **is** the *possibility* of prior *approval* of it.	=	He *may* **approve** of it ahead of time.
We **conducted** an *investigation* of it.	=	We **investigated** it.
A *review* **was done** of the regulations.	=	They **reviewed** the regulations

There is a technical term for a noun derived from a verb or an adjective. It is called a *nominalization.* Nominalization is itself a noun derived from a verb, *nominalize.* Here are some examples:

Verb →	Nominalization	Adjective →	Nominalization
discover	discovery	careless	carelessness
move	movement	difficult	difficulty
resist	resistance	different	difference
react	reaction	elegant	elegance
fail	failure	applicable	applicability
refuse	refusal	intense	intensity

Some nominalizations are identical to their corresponding verb: *hope → hope, charge → charge, result → result, answer → answer, repair → repair, return → return.*

Our **request** is that on your **return,** you conduct a **review** of the data and provide an immediate **report.**

We **request** that when you **return,** you **review** the data and **report** immediately.

Nominalization might sound like jargon, but it's a useful term.

Looking for Nominalizations

A few patterns of useless nominalizations are easy to spot and revise.

1. When the nominalization follows a verb with little specific meaning, change the nominalization to a verb that can replace the empty verb.

> The police *conducted* an **investigation** into the matter.
> The police *investigated* the matter.

> The committee *has* no **expectation** that it will meet the deadline.
> The committee does not *expect* to meet the deadline.

2. When the nominalization follows *there is* or *there are,* change the nominalization to a verb and find a subject:

> *There* is a **need** for further **study** of this program.
> *The engineering staff* **must study** this program further.

> *There was* considerable **erosion** of the land from the floods.
> *The floods* considerably **eroded** the land.

3. When the nominalization is the subject of an empty verb, change the nominalization to a verb and find a new subject:

> The **intention** of the IRS *is* to audit the records of the program.
> The IRS **intends** to audit the records of the program.

> *Our* **discussion** *concerned* a tax cut.
> *We* **discussed** a tax cut.

4. When you find consecutive nominalizations, turn the first one into a verb. Then either leave the second or turn it into a verb in a clause beginning with *how* or *why:*

> There was first a **review** of the **evolution** of the dorsal fin.
> First, she **reviewed** the **evolution** of the dorsal fin.
> First, she **reviewed** *how* the dorsal fin **evolved.**

5. We have to revise more extensively when a nominalization in a subject is linked to a second nominalization in the predicate by a verb or phrase that logically connects them:

Subject:	Their **cessation** of hostilities
Logical connection:	was because of
Object:	their personnel **losses.**

To revise such sentences,

(a) Change abstractions to verbs: *cessation* → *cease, loss* → *lose.*

(b) Find subjects for those verbs: ***they ceased,*** ***they lost.***

(c) Link the new clauses with a word that expresses their logical connection. That connection will typically be some kind of causal relationship;

To express simple cause:	*because, since, when*
To express conditional cause:	*if, provided that, so long as*
To contradict expected cause:	*though, although, unless.*

Schematically, we do this:

Their **cessation** of hostilities	→	they **ceased** hostilities
was because of	→	because
their personnel **loss**	→	they **lost** personnel

More examples:

The **discovery** of a method for the **manufacture** of artificial skin *will have the result* of an **increase** in the **survival** of patients with radical burns.

—Researchers **discover** how to **manufacture** artificial skin
—More patients **will survive** radical burns

If researchers **can discover** how to **manufacture** artificial skin, more patients **will survive** radical burns.

The presence of extensive rust **damage** to exterior surfaces *prevented* immediate **repairs** to the hull.

—Rust had extensively **damaged** the exterior surfaces
—We could not **repair** the hull immediately

Because rust had extensively **damaged** the exterior surfaces, we could not **repair** the hull immediately.

The **instability** of the motor housing *did not preclude* the **completion** of the field trials.

—The motor housing was **unstable**
—The research staff **completed** field trials

Even though the motor housing **was unstable,** the research staff **completed** the field trials.

Useful Nominalizations

In some cases, nominalizations are useful, even necessary. Don't revise these.

1. The nominalization is a subject referring to a previous sentence:

> **These arguments** all depend on a single unproven claim.
> **This decision** can lead to costly consequences.

These nominalizations let us link sentences into a more cohesive flow.

2. The nominalization names what would be the object of its verb:

> I do not understand either **her meaning** or **his intention**.

This is a bit more compact than, "I do not understand either **what she means** or **what he intends**."

3. A succinct nominalization can replace an awkward "The fact that":

> **The fact that I denied what he accused me of** impressed the jury.
> **My denial of his accusations** impressed the jury.

But then, why not

> When I **denied** his accusations, I **impressed** the jury.

4. Some nominalizations refer to an often repeated concept.

> Few issues have so divided Americans as **abortion on demand**.
>
> The Equal Rights **Amendment** was an issue in past **elections**.
>
> **Taxation** without **representation** was not the central concern of the American **Revolution**.

In these sentences, the nominalization names concepts that we refer to repeatedly: *abortion on demand, Amendment, election, taxation, representation, Revolution*. Rather than repeatedly spell out a familiar concept in a full clause, we contract it into a noun. In these cases, the abstractions often become virtual actors.

And, of course, some nominalizations refer to ideas that we can express only in nominalizations: *freedom, death, love, hope, life, wisdom*. If we couldn't turn some verbs or adjectives into nouns, we would find it difficult—perhaps impossible—to discuss those subjects that have preoccupied us for millennia. You simply have to develop an eye—or an ear—for the nominalization that expresses one of these ideas and the nominalization that hides a significant action:

There is a **demand** for an **end** to **taxation** on **entertainment.**

We **demand** that the government **stop taxing entertainment.**

5. We often use a nominalization after *there is/are* to introduce a topic that we develop in subsequent sentences (as distinct from an isolated *there is* + nominalization, see p. 31):

> *There is* no **need,** then, for **argument** about the **existence,** the **inevitability,** and the **desirability** of **change** [in language]. *There is* **need,** however, for **argument** about the **existence** of such a thing as good English and correct English. Let us not hesitate to assert that "The pencil was laying on the table" and "He don't know nothing" are at present incorrect no matter how many know-nothings say them. Let us insist that . . . Let us demand that . . . Let us do these things not to satisfy "rules" or to gratify the whims of a pedagogue, but rather to express ourselves clearly, precisely, logically, and directly.
> —Theodore M. Bernstein, *The Careful Writer*[4]

(Of course, we might also consider revising those first two sentences into "Language changes, and such changes are both inevitable and sometimes desirable. But there is such a thing as good English and correct English.")

6. And sometimes our topic seems so abstract that we think we can write about it only in nominalizations. Here are two passages about an abstract principle of law. In the first, the abstract nominalization *recovery in equity* acts virtually as a character. It "requires," it "recovers," it "relaxes," just as a real character might.

> In comparison to the statutory method of recovery, there are certain advantages in the equitable right of recovery. **Recovery in equity** does not require strict compliance with statutory requirements. Because **equitable recovery** can be tailored to the particular controversy, it allows one to recover greater or lesser amounts. **A statutory action for the recovery of rents** can recover only the value of use and occupation exclusive of improvements to the property. **An equity action,** on the other hand, can recover rents based upon the value of the property with the defendant's improvements thereupon. **Proceedings in equity** also relax the evidentiary standard. Most importantly, unlike the statutory method, **recovery in equity** does not demand one year of possession prior to suit. **Both statutory and equitable remedies,** however, require the same standard of good faith.

But we can explain the same concepts using subject/characters and verb/actions.

> In comparison to the statutory method, **a plaintiff** will find certain advantages through an equitable right of recovery. In recovery in equity, **the plaintiff** need not strictly comply with statutory requirements. Because **he** can tailor recovery to the equities of the controversy, **he** may be able to recover greater or lesser amounts. In a statutory action regarding the recovery of rents, **a plaintiff** can recover only the value of use and occupation exclusive of improvements to the property. On the other hand, under recovery in equity, **the plaintiff** can recover rents based upon the value of the property with the defendant's improvements thereupon. In proceedings in equity, **the court** may also relax the evidentiary standard. Most importantly, unlike the statutory method, in recovery in equity **the plaintiff** does not have to possess the land one year prior to suit. In both statutory and equitable remedies, however, **the court** requires the same standard of good faith.

Other passages do not lend themselves to revision so easily (I boldface the nominalizations and italicize the characters).

> The **argument** is this. The cognitive component of **intention** exhibits a high degree of **complexity**. **Intention** is temporally divisible into two: prospective **intention** and immediate **intention**. The cognitive **function** of prospective **intention** is the **representation** of a *subject's* similar past **actions**, *his* current situation, and *his* course of future **actions**. That is, the cognitive component of prospective **intention** is a **plan**. The cognitive **function** of immediate **intention** is the **monitoring** and **guidance** of ongoing bodily **movement**. Taken together these cognitive mechanisms are highly complex. The folk psychological notion of **belief**, however, is an attitude that permits limited **complexity** of content. Thus the cognitive component of **intention** is something other than folk psychological **belief**.
> —Myles Brand, *Intending and Acting*[5]

Translated into an agent-action style, this passage loses something of its generality, some would say its philosophical import. Only its author could judge whether our translation has misrepresented his argument.

> I argue like this: When *an actor* **intends** anything, *he* **behaves** in ways that are cognitively complex. *We* **may divide** these ways into two temporal modes: *He* **intends** prospectively or immediately.

When *an actor* **intends** prospectively, *he* cognitively **represents** to himself what *he* **has done** similarly in the past, his current situation, and how *he* **intends** to **act** in the future. That is, when *an actor* **intends** prospectively, *he* **plans.** On the other hand, when *an actor* **plans** what *he* **intends** to **do** immediately, *he* **monitors** and **guides** his body as *he* **moves** it. When *we* **take** these two cognitive components together, *we* **see** that **they are highly complex. But** *our* beliefs about these matters on the basis of folk psychology are too simple. When *we* **consider** the cognitive component of intention in this way, *we* **see** that *we* **have** to **think** in ways other than folk psychology.

This passage illustrates the problem with finding an impersonal subject. Should we/one/the writer/you use as subjects *we, one, he, philosophers, anyone?*

Passives and Agents

In addition to avoiding abstract nominalizations, you can make your style more direct if you also avoid unnecessary passive verbs. In active sentences, the subject typically expresses the agent of an action, and the object expresses the goal or the thing changed by the action:

subject   object

Active: The partners → broke → the agreement.

agent   goal

In passive sentences, the subject expresses the goal of an action; a form of *be* precedes a past participle form of the verb; and the agent of the action may or may not be expressed in a *by*-phrase:

               be (past   prepositional

subject   participle)   phrase

Passive: The agreement ← was broken ← by the partners.

goal   agent

We can usually make our style more vigorous and direct if we avoid both nominalizations and unnecessary passive verbs. Compare:

A new approach to toxic waste management detailed in a chemical industry plan **will be submitted.** A method of decomposing toxic by-products of refinery processes **has been discovered** by Genco Chemical.

The chemical industry **will submit** a plan that details a new way to manage toxic waste. Genco Chemical **has discovered** a way to decompose toxic by-products of refinery processes.

Active sentences encourage us to name the specific agent of an action and avoid a few extra words—a form of *be* and, when we preserve the Agent of the action, the preposition *by*. Because the passive also reverses the direct order of agent-action-goal, passives eventually cripple the easy flow of an otherwise energetic style. Compare these passages:

> It **was found** that data concerning energy resources allocated to the states **were not obtained.** This action **is needed** so that a determination of redirection **is permitted** on a timely basis when weather conditions change. A system **must be established** so that data on weather conditions and fuel consumption **may be gathered** on a regular basis.

> We **found** that the Department of Energy **did not obtain** data about energy resources that Federal offices **were allocating** to the states. The Department **needs** these data so that it **can determine** how to **redirect** these resources when conditions **change.** The Secretary of the Department **must establish** a system so that his office **can gather** data on weather conditions and fuel consumption on a regular basis.

The second passage is a bit longer, but more specific and more straightforward. We know who is supposed to be doing what.

When we combine passives with nominalizations, we create that wretched prose we call legalese, sociologicalese, educationalese, bureaucratese—all of the *-eses* of those who confuse authority and objectivity with polysyllabic abstraction and remote impersonality:

> Patient movement to less restrictive methods of care may be followed by increased probability of recovery.

> If we treat patients less restrictively, they may recover faster.

But those are the easy generalizations. In many other cases, we may find that the passive is, in fact, the better choice.

Choosing between Active and Passive

To choose between the active and the passive, we have to answer two questions: First, must our audience know who is performing the action? Second, are we maintaining a logically consistent string of subjects? And third, if the string of subjects is consistent, is it the right string of subjects?

Often, we avoid stating who is responsible for an action, because we don't know or don't care, or because we'd just rather not say:

> Those who **are found** guilty of murder **can be executed.**

> Valuable records **should always be kept** in a fireproof safe.

In sentences like these, the passive is the natural and correct choice. In this next sentence, we might also predict the passive, but for a different reason, one having to do with avoiding responsibility:

> Because the final safety inspection **was** neither **performed** nor **monitored,** the brake plate assembly mechanism **was left** incorrectly aligned, a fact that **was known** several months before it **was decided** to publicly reveal that information.

This kind of writing raises issues more significant than mere clarity.

The second consideration is more complex: it is whether the subjects in a sequence of sentences are consistent. Look again at the subjects in the pair of paragraphs about energy (p. 37). In the first version, the subjects of the passive sentences seem to be chosen almost at random.

> It . . . information . . . This action . . . a determination . . . A system . . . information. . . .

In the second, the active sentences give the reader a consistent point of view; the writer "stages" the sentences from a consistent string of subjects, in this case the agents of the action:

> We . . . Department of Energy . . . Federal offices . . . the Department . . . it . . . the Secretary . . . his office. . . .

Now each agent-subject anchors the reader in something familiar at the beginning of the sentence—the cast of characters—before the reader moves on to something new.

If in a series of passive sentences, you find yourself shifting from one unrelated subject to another, try rewriting those sentences in the active voice. Use the beginning of your sentence to orient your reader to what follows. If in a series of sentences you give your reader no consistent starting point, then that stretch of writing may well seem disjointed.

If, however, you can make your sequence of subjects appropriately consistent, then choose the passive. In this next passage, the writer wanted to write about the end of World War II from the point of view of Germany and Japan. So in each of her sentences, she put Germany and Japan into the subject of a verb, regardless of whether the verb was active or passive:

> By March of 1945, **the Axis nations** had been essentially defeated; all that remained was a final, but bloody, climax. The **borders of Germany** had been breached, and **both Germany and Japan** were being bombed around the clock. **Neither country,** though, had been so devastated that it could not resist.

If, however, she had wanted to write about the end of the war from the point of view of the Allied nations, she would have chosen the active:

> By March of 1945, **the Allies** had essentially defeated the Axis nations; all that remained was a final, but bloody, climax. **American, French, and British forces** had breached the borders of Germany and were bombing both Germany and Japan around the clock. But **they** had not so thoroughly devastated either country as to destroy its ability to resist.

We will return to this matter in Chapter 3.

The Institutional Passive

When we try to revise passives in official and academic prose, we often run into a problem, because many editors and teachers believe that passages such as the following are stylistically improper (each comes from the opening of articles published in quite respectable journals):

> This paper is concerned with two problems. How can **we** best handle, in a transformational grammar (i) Restrictions. . . . To illustrate (i), **we** may cite . . . **we** shall show . . .

> Since the pituitary-adrenal axis is activated during the acute phase response, **we** have investigated the potential role . . . Specifically, **we** have studied the effects of interleukin-1 . . .

> Any study of tensions presupposes some acquaintance with certain findings of child psychology. **We** may begin by inquiring whether . . . **we** should next proceed to investigate.

Here are the first few words from several consecutive sentences in an article in *Science,* a journal of substantial prestige:

> . . . we want . . . Survival gives . . . We examine . . . . We compare . . . . We have used . . . . Each has been weighted . . . . We merely take . . . . They are subject . . . . We use . . . . Efron and Morris (3) describe . . . . We observed . . . . We might find . . . . We know. . . .[6]

Certainly, scholars in different fields write in different ways. And in all fields, some scholarly writers and editors resolutely avoid the first person everywhere. But if they claim that all good academic writing in all fields must always be impersonally third-person, always passive, they are wrong.

Metadiscourse: Writing about Writing

We now must explain, however, that when academic and scholarly writers do use the first person, they use it for particular purposes. Note the verbs in the passages cited: *cite, show, begin by inquiring, compare.* The writers are referring to their acts of writing or arguing, and are using what we shall call *metadiscourse.*

Metadiscourse is the language we use when, in writing about some subject matter, we incidentally refer to the act and to the context of writing about it. We use metadiscourse verbs to announce that in what follows we will *explain, show, argue, claim, deny, describe, suggest, contrast, add, expand, summarize.* We use metadiscourse to list the parts or steps in our presentation: *first, second, third, finally;* to express our logical connections: *infer, support, prove, illustrate, therefore, in conclusion, however, on the other hand.* We hedge how certain we are by writing *it seems that, perhaps, I believe, probably,* etc. Though metadiscourse does not refer to what we are primarily saying about our subject, we need some metadiscourse in everything we write.

If scholarly writers use the first person at all, they predictably use *I* or *we* in introductions, where they announce their intentions in metadiscourse: *We claim that, We shall show, We begin by examining.* If writers use metadiscourse at the beginning of a piece, they often use it again at the end, when they review what they have done: *We have suggested, I have shown that, We have, however, not claimed.* Less often, scholarly writers use the first person to refer to their most general actions involved in researching their problem. This is not metadiscourse when it applies to the acts of research: *we investigate, study, examine, compare, know, analyze, review, evaluate, assess, find, discover.*

Academic and scientific writers rarely use the first person when they refer to particular actions. We are unlikely to find passages such as this:

> To determine if monokines directly elicited an adrenal steroidogenic response, **I added** monocyte-conditioned medium and purified preparations of . . .

Far more likely is the original sentence:

> To determine if monokines directly elicited an adrenal steroidogenic response, **monocyte-conditioned medium and purified preparations . . . were added** to cultures . . .

Note that when the writer wrote this sentence in the passive, he unselfconsciously dangled his modifier:

> To determine . . . medium and purified preparations were added . . .

The implied subject of the verb *determine* is *I* or *we; I determine.* But that implied subject *I* or *we* differs from *medium and purified preparations,* the explicit subject of the main verb *added.* And thus dangles the modifier: the implied subject of the introductory phrase differs from the explicit subject of the clause.

Writers of scientific prose use this pattern so often that it has become standard usage in scientific English. The few editors who have stern views on these matters object, of course. But if they do, they must accept first-person subjects. If they both deprive their authors of a first-person subject and rule out dangling modifiers, they put their writers into a damned-if-you-do, damned-if-you-don't predicament.

As a small historical footnote, we might add that this impersonal "scientific" style is a modern development. In his "New Theory of Light and Colors" (1672), Sir Isaac Newton wrote this rather charming account of an early experiment:

> I procured a triangular glass prism, to try therewith the celebrated phenomena of colors. And for that purpose, having darkened my laboratory, and made a small hole in my window shade, to let in a convenient quantity of the sun's light, I placed my prism at the entrance, that the light might be thereby refracted to the opposite

wall. It was at first a very pleasing diversion to view the vivid and intense colors produced thereby.

Noun + Noun + Noun

A last habit of style that often keep us from making the connections between our ideas explicit is the unnecessarily long compound noun phrase:

> **Early childhood thought disorder misdiagnosis** often occurs because of unfamiliarity with recent **research literature** describing such conditions. This paper reviews seven recent studies of particular relevance to **preteen hyperactivity diagnosis** and to **treatment modalities** involving **medication maintenance level evaluation procedures.**

Some grammarians insist that we should never use one noun to modify another, but that would rule out common phrases like *stone wall* or *student committee.* And if we ruled out such phrases, writers of technical prose would be unable to compact into a single phrase complex thoughts that they would otherwise have to repeat in longer constructions. If a writer must refer several times in an article to the idea behind *medication maintenance level evaluation procedures,* then repeating that phrase is marginally better than repeating *procedures to evaluate ways to maintain levels of medication.* In less technical writing, though, compounds like these seem awkward or, worse, ambiguous, especially when they include nominalizations.

So, whenever you find in your writing a string of nouns that you have never read before and that you probably will not use again, try disassembling them. Start from the last and reverse their order, even linking them with prepositional phrases, if necessary. If one of the nouns is a nominalization, change it into a verb. Here is the first compound in the example passage revised:

$$1 \qquad 2 \qquad 3 \qquad 4$$
early childhood thought disorder misdiagnosis

$$4 \qquad 3 \qquad 2 \qquad 1$$
→ misdiagnose disordered thought in early childhood

(Now we can see the ambiguity: what's early, the childhood, the disorder, or the diagnosis?) Then reassemble into a sentence:

Physicians are misdiagnosing disordered thought in young children because they are not familiar with the literature on recent research.

Summing Up

1. Express actions and conditions in specific verbs, adverbs, or adjectives:

The **intention** of the committee is the **improvement** of morale.

The committee **intends** to **improve** morale.

2. When appropriate, make the subjects of your verbs characters involved in those actions.

A decision on the part of **the Dean** about funding by **the Department** of its program must be made for there to be adequate **staff** preparation.

If **the staff** is to prepare adequately, **the Dean** must decide whether **the Department** will fund the program.

We can sum up these principles in the diagram we offered on p. 26.

FIXED	SUBJECT	VERB	COMPLEMENT
VARIABLE	CHARACTERS	ACTION	———

To the degree that we consistently expresses the crucial actions of our story in verbs and our central characters (real or abstract) in subjects, our readers are likely to feel our prose is clear and direct. This, however, is only the first step toward clear, direct, and *coherent* writing.

Well begun is half done.
Anonymous

The two capital secrets in the art of prose composition are these:
first the philosophy of transition and connection; or the art by
which one step in an evolution of thought is made to arise out of
another: all fluent and effective composition depends on the con-
nections; secondly, the way in which sentences are made to
modify each other; for the most powerful effects in written elo-
quence arise out of this reverberation, as it were, from each
other in a rapid succession of sentences.
Thomas De Quincy

"Begin at the beginning," the King said, gravely, "and go on till
you come to the end; then stop."
Lewis Carroll

3

Cohesion

Clarity and Context

So far, we've discussed clear writing as if we wrote only individual sentences, independent of context or intention; as if we could directly map onto subjects and verbs the way characters and actions appear to us as we directly experience the world. And it's true—if we mechanically arranged characters and their apparent actions so that they matched subjects and verbs, we would achieve a kind of local clarity.

But there is more to readable writing than local clarity. A series of clear sentences can still be confusing if we fail to design them to fit their context, to reflect a consistent point of view, to emphasize our most important ideas. These sentences could all refer to the same set of conditions, but each leads us to understand the conditions from a different point of view.

> Congress finally agreed with the Secretary of State that if we ally ourselves with Saudi Arabia and Iran then attacks Kuwait, we will have to protect Kuwait.

> The Secretary of State finally convinced Congress that if Kuwait comes under Iranian attack, it will need our protection if Saudi Arabia has acquired us as an ally.

> The Secretary of State and Congress finally agreed that if we and Saudi Arabia become allies and Kuwait and Iran enter into hostilities initiated by Iran, then we and Kuwait will become allies in the hostilities.

The problem is to discover how, without sacrificing local clarity, we can shape sentences to fit their context and to reflect those larger intentions that motivate us to write in the first place.

In Chapters 1 and 2, we began explaining matters of style by trying first to refine the way we describe our responses to different kinds of prose. In those chapters, we described passages such as the next one as "turgid" or "murky" (still keeping in mind that in fact we are describing not the prose but our feelings about it):

> 1a. To obligate a corporation upon a contract to another party, it must be proven that the contract was its act, whether by corporate action, that of an authorized agent, or by adoption or ratification and such ratification will be implied by the acquiescence or the acceptance of the benefits of such contract, it being essential to implied ratification that the acceptance be with knowledge of all pertinent facts.

Once we are aware of how we feel about a passage like this and conscious of the words we can use to describe those feelings, we know how to begin analyzing the passage so that we can revise it. First, who are the characters? Then what actions are they performing? To revise, we name the characters in subjects and actions in verbs:

> 1b. To prove that a **corporation** *is obligated* to another party, **the other party** *must prove* one of two conditions:
>   - **the corporation or its authorized agent** explicitly *acted* to *enter* the contract, or
>   - **the corporation** *adopted* or implicitly *ratified* the contract when, knowing all pertinent facts, it *acquiesced* in or *accepted* its benefits.

Now read this next pair of passages. How would you describe their differences?

> 2a. Asian competitors who have sought to compete directly with Acme's X-line product groups in each of six market segments in the Western Pacific region will constitute the main objective of the first phase of this study. The labor costs of Acme's competitors and their ability to introduce new products quickly define the issue we will examine in detail in each segment. A plan that will show Acme how to restructure its diverse and widespread facilities so that it can better exploit unexpected opportunities, particularly in the market on the Pacific Rim, should result.

> 2b. The first phase of this study will mainly examine six market segments in the Western Pacific region to determine how Asian competitors have sought to compete directly with Acme's X-line product groups. In each segment, the study will examine in detail their labor costs and their ability to in-

troduce new products quickly. The result will be a plan that will show Acme how to restructure its diverse and widespread facilities so that it can better exploit unexpected opportunities, particularly in the market on the Pacific Rim.

Passage (2b) is "clearer" than (2a), but to describe how it is clearer and what makes it so, we would have to use words different from those we used to describe the passages about corporate contracts. Neither (2a) nor (2b) has any problems with nominalizations; both have about the same number of characters as subjects of verbs. So (2a) is not more "turgid," "abstract," or "complex" than (2b). Most readers have described the first as "disjointed," "abrupt," "choppy," as lacking in "flow"; (2b) as "flowing," "connected," and "cohesive."

This chapter will explain these responses and suggest how to revise a passage like (2a) into a passage like (2b).

Managing the Flow of Information

Few principles of style are more widely repeated than "use the direct active voice, avoid the weak and indirect passive." Not

a. A black hole **is created** by the collapse of a dead star into a point perhaps no larger than a marble.

but rather,

b. The collapse of a dead star into a point perhaps no larger than a marble **creates** a black hole.

But what if the context for either of those sentences was this:

(1) Some astonishing questions about the nature of the universe have been raised by scientists exploring the nature of black holes in space. (2a/b) —— (3) So much matter compressed into so little volume changes the fabric of space around it in profoundly puzzling ways.

Our sense of coherence should tell us that this context calls not for the active sentence, but for the passive. And the reasons are not far to seek: The last part of sentence (1) introduces one of the important characters in the story: black holes in space. If we write sentence (2) in the active voice, we cannot mention black holes again until its end, as the object of an active verb:

(2b) The collapse of a dead star . . . **creates** a black hole.

We can improve the flow between sentences (1) and (2) if we shift that object in sentence (2)—a black hole—to the beginning of its own sentence, where it will echo the last few words of sentence (1). We can do that by making *black hole* the subject of a passive verb:

> the nature of black holes in space. A black hole is created by the collapse of a dead star (or . . . when a dead star collapses).

By doing that, we also move to the end of sentence (2) the concept that will open sentence (3), and thereby create a tight conceptual link between those two sentences:

> the nature of black holes in space. A black hole is created by the collapse of a dead star into a point perhaps no larger than a marble. So much matter compressed into so little volume changes the fabric of space. . . .

The problem—and the challenge—of English prose is that, with every sentence we write, we have to strike the best compromise between the principles of local clarity and directness that we discussed in Chapter 2, and the principles of cohesion that fuse separate sentences into a whole discourse. But in that compromise, we must give priority to those features of style that make our discourse seem cohesive, those features that help the reader organize separate sentences into a single, unified whole.

We've illustrated two complementary principles of cohesion. One of them is this:

> Put at the beginning of a sentence those ideas that you have already mentioned, referred to, or implied, or concepts that you can reasonably assume your reader is already familiar with, and will readily recognize.

The other principle is this:

> Put at the end of your sentence the newest, the most surprising, the most significant information: information that you want to stress—perhaps the information that you will expand on in your next sentence.

As you begin a sentence, you have to prepare your readers for new and therefore important information. Give your readers a familiar context to help them move from the more familiar to the less familiar, from the known to the unknown.

All of us recognize this principle when a good teacher tries to teach us something new. That teacher will always try to connect something we already know to whatever new we are trying to learn. Sentences work in the same way. Each sentence should teach your reader something new. To lead your reader to whatever will seem new *to that reader,* you have to begin that sentence with something that you can reasonably assume *that reader* already knows. How you begin sentences, then, is crucial to how easily your readers will understand them, not individually, but as they constitute a whole passage. But in designing sentences in this way, you must have some sense of what your reader already knows about your subject.

Beginning Well

It's harder to begin a sentence well than to end it well. As we'll see later, to end a sentence well, we need only decide which of our ideas is the newest, probably the most complex, and then imagine that complex idea at the end of its own sentence. The problem is merely to get there gracefully. On the other hand, every time we begin a sentence, we have to juggle three or four elements that typically occur early on.

1. To connect a sentence to the preceding one, we use transitional metadiscourse, such as *and, but, therefore, as a result—* And therefore . . . .

2. To help readers evaluate what follows, we use expressions such as *fortunately, perhaps, allegedly, it is important to note, for the most part, under these circumstances, from a practical point of view, politically speaking.*

> And therefore, **it is important to note, that from a practical point of view.** . . .

3. We locate action in time and place: *then, later, on May 23, in Europe.*

> And therefore, it is important to note, that from a practical point of view, **in the Northeastern states in recent years.** . . .

4. And most important (note the evaluation), we announce at the beginning of a sentence its *topic*—the concept that we intend to say something about. We ordinarily name the topic of a sentence or clause in its subject:

> And therefore, it is important to note, that from a practical point of view, in the Northeastern states in recent years, **these sources of acid rain** have been a matter of much concern. . . .

Your style will seem cohesive to the degree that you can subordinate the first three of the elements that open a sentence to the fourth, to its topic. If you begin sentences with the kind of throat-clearing introduction of the sentence above, your prose will seem not just uncertain, but unfocused. We will begin with topics, because they are centrally important in the ways readers read.

Topics: Psychological Subjects

The topic of a sentence is its *psychological* subject. The psychological subject of a sentence is that idea we announce in the first few words of a sentence. It is almost always a noun phrase of some kind that the rest of the sentence characterizes, comments on, says something about. In most English sentences, psychological subjects (topics), are also grammatical subjects:

> **Private higher education** is seriously concerned about population trends through the end of the century.

The writer first announces the grammatical subject, *Private higher education*. As readers, we assume the writer is going to comment on, say something about that concept. In this sense, the sentence is "about" private higher education.

But we can create a topic out of the object of a verb if we shift that object to the beginning of its sentence, before the subject:

> I cannot explain **the reasons for this decision to end the treaty.**

> **The reasons for this decision to end the treaty,** I cannot explain.

We can also put topics in introductory phrases:

> As for **abortion,** it is not clear how the Supreme Court will rule.

> In regard to **regulating religious cults,** we must proceed cautiously.

Neither *abortion* nor *regulating religious cults* is the subject of its sentence. The main subject of the first is *it,* and of the second, *we.* If we ask what either of those sentences is really "about," we would not say that the sentences were "about" their grammatical subjects, *it* or *we.* Those sentences are "about" their psychological subjects, their topics—abortion, and regulating religious cults.

Here's the point. In the clearest writing, the topics of most sentences and clauses are their grammatical subjects. But what's more important than their grammatical function is the way top-ics control how readers read sentences, not individually, but in sequences, and the way that writers must therefore organize *sequences* of those topics. The most important concern of a writer, then, is not the individual topics of individual sentences, but the cumulative effect of the sequence of topics.

The Role of Topics

In this paragraph, **boldface** indicate topics. **Particular ideas toward the beginning of each clause** define what a passage is centrally "about" for a reader, so **a sense of coherence** crucially depends on topics. Cumulatively, **the thematic signposts that are provided by these ideas** should focus the reader's attention toward a well-defined and limited set of connected ideas. **Moving through a paragraph from a cumulatively coherent point of view** is made possible by a sequence of topics that seem to constitute this coherent sequence of topicalized ideas. **A seeming absence of context for each sentence** is one consequence of making random shifts in topics. **Feelings of dislocation, disorientation, and lack of focus** will occur when **that** happens. **The seeming coherence of whole sections** will turn on a reader's point of view as a result of topic announcement.

Compare that with this.

In this paragraph, I have boldfaced the topics of every clause. **Topics** are crucial for a reader because **they** focus the reader's attention on a particular idea toward the beginning of a clause and thereby notify a reader what **a clause** is "about." **Topics** thereby crucially determine whether **the reader** will feel **a passage** is coherent. Cumulatively, through a series of sentences, **these topicalized ideas** provide thematic signposts that focus the reader's attention on a well-defined set of connected ideas. If **a sequence of topics** seems coherent, **that consistent sequence** will move the reader through a paragraph from a cumulatively coherent point of view. But if through that paragraph **topics** shift randomly, then **the reader** has to begin each sentence out of context, from no coherent point of view. When **that** happens, **the reader** will feel dislocated, disoriented, out of focus. **Whatever the writer announces**

as a topic, then, will fix the reader's point of view, not just toward the rest of the sentence, but toward whole sections.

To most readers the original has no consistent focus, no consistent string of topics that focuses attention on a circumscribed set of concepts. So, as most readers feel dislocated, disoriented, or unfocused, they describe the passage as disjointed, choppy, lacking in "flow." The revised version consistently focuses on fewer concepts: for the most part, some variation on *topics* and *reader*. It has a more consistent *topic string,* and therefore feels more focused, more cohesive.

This principle of a coherent topic string also helps us understand why we can be confused by one long sentence after another. Long sentences may not announce topics often enough or clearly enough to guide us through a multitude of ideas. We need topics as thematic signposts to help us assemble ideas in individual sentences and clauses into cohesive discourse.

This principle of using a consistent string of topics reinforces a point we made about characters and actions: When you design your sentences so that their subjects predictably name your central characters—real or abstract—and the verbs in those sentences name crucial actions, you are beginning your sentences from a point of view your readers will feel is consistent, from the point of view of your characters, the most familiar units of information in any story you tell. In fact, we can expand the graphic model that we offered in the last chapter:

TOPIC			FIXED
OLD INFORMATION	NEW INFORMATION		VARIABLE
SUBJECT	VERB	—	FIXED
CHARACTERS	ACTION	—	VARIABLE

The secret to a clear and readable style is in the first five or six words of every sentence. At the beginning of every sentence, locate your reader in familiar territory; at the beginning of a series of sentences, create for your reader a reasonably consistent point of view, a consistent topic string. When that consistent topic string consists of your cast of characters as subjects, and you immediately connect those subjects with verbs that express the crucial actions, you are a long way toward writing prose that your readers will perceive as clear, direct, and cohesive.

Keeping Topics Visible

We can now appreciate why a writer has to get most of his or her sentences off to a brisk start with an appropriate topic. We fail to do this when we introduce sentences with too much metadiscourse, that language we use when we write about our own writing or thinking. These next sentences appeared in a study of a college curriculum. I have italicized the metadiscourse and bold-faced what I believe should have been the topics.

> *We think it useful to provide some relatively detailed illustration of* the varied ways "corporate curricular personalities" organize themselves in **programs**. *We choose to feature as a central device in our presentation what are called* "introductory," "survey," or "foundational" courses. *It is important, however, to recognize* the diversity of what occurs in **programs** after the different initial survey courses. *But what is also suggested is that if one talks about* a **program** *simply in terms of* the intellectual strategies or techniques engaged in, when these *are understood in a general way,* it becomes difficult to distinguish many programs from others.

Get rid of the metadiscourse, make the central character—programs—the topic, and we get a substantially more compelling claim:

> **Our programs** create varied "corporate" curricular personalities, particularly through their "introductory," "survey," or "foundational" courses. After these initial courses, **they** continue to offer diverse curricula. *But* in these curricula **they** seem to employ similar intellectual strategies.

At this point, some of you may be recalling advice that you once received about avoiding "monotony"—vary how you begin your sentences, avoid beginning sentences with the same subjects. Bad advice.

Your prose will become monotonous for reasons more serious than repeated topics or subjects. It will be monotonous if you write one short sentence after another, or one long sentence after another. Your prose will seem monotonous if you stuff it with nominalizations and passives.

You avoid monotony by saying what you have to say as clearly as you can, by so thoroughly engaging your readers in your ideas that they lose touch with the surface of your prose. Under any circumstances, because we ordinarily write "stories" with several different characters, we are unlikely to repeat the same words for the same characters at the beginning of several consecutive sentences. And even if we do, most readers will not notice.

At the risk of asking a question that might invite the wrong answer, did the revised paragraph about topics, the one with the consistent topics, seem more monotonous than the original (p. 51)? It has only two main topics: *topics* and *reader*. If, as you read the paragraph, your eyes did not glaze over (as a result of the prose style, at any rate), then we have settled the issue of monotony and consistent subjects.

Managing Subjects and Topics for Flow

English provides us with several ways to replace a long subject that expresses new information with a shorter segment that probably expresses information repeated from or referring to a previous sentence. Notice how, in each of the example sentences below, we move to the end a long subject that expresses new and therefore relatively more important information. Note as well that the shorter segment which we move to the beginning expresses older information, information that typically connects the reader to something that has gone before.

Passives again. As we have seen, an important role of the passive is to let us replace a long subject full of new information with a short one that locates the reader in the context of something more familiar:

> During the first years of our nation, *a series of brilliant and virtuous presidents committed to a democratic republic yet confident in their own superior worth* conducted **its administration.**

> During the first years of our nation, **its administration** was conducted by *a series of brilliant and virtuous presidents committed to a democratic republic yet confident in their own superior worth.*

Astronomers, physicists, and a host of other researchers entirely familiar with the problems raised by quasars have confirmed **these observations.**

These observations have been confirmed by *astronomers, physicists, and a host of other researchers entirely familiar with the problems raised by quasars.*

These sentences illustrate the main reason the passive exists in the language—to improve cohesion and emphasis.

Subject-complement switching. Sometimes, we simply switch the subject and complement, especially when what follows the linking verb *be* refers to something already mentioned:

The source of the American attitude toward rural dialects is **more interesting** [than something already mentioned].

More interesting [than something already mentioned] is *the source of the American attitude toward rural dialects.*

We can make a similar switch with a few other verbs:

The failure of the administration to halt the rising costs of hospital care lies **at the heart of the problem.**

At the heart of the problem lies *the failure of the administration to halt the rising costs of hospital care.*

Some complex issues run **through these questions.**

Through these questions run *some complex issues.*

Subject-Clause Transformations. If you have a very long subject that does not allow you simply to switch it to the end of the clause, you can occasionally turn it into an introductory clause, allowing you to construct two shorter topics (subjects are boldfaced):

An attorney who uncovers after the close of a discovery proceeding documents that might be even peripherally relevant to a matter involved in the discovery proceeding must notify both the court and the opposing attorney immediately.

[*If* **a discovery proceeding** closes and **an attorney** then uncovers documents that might be even peripherally relevant to the matter of the proceeding,] **he** must notify both the court and the opposing attorney immediately.

Two Principles

Here are two principles that are more important than getting characters into the subjects of your sentences.

1. Put in the subject/topic of your sentences ideas that you have already mentioned, or ideas that are so familiar to your reader that if you state them at the beginning of a sentence, you will not surprise anyone.
2. Among groups of related sentences, keep their topics consistent, if you can. They don't have to be identical, but they should constitute a string that your readers will take to be focused.

Here are two consequences:

1. You may find yourself writing as many passive sentences as active. But if active sentences create a less consistent string of topics, leave the sentences passive.
2. You may find yourself using nominalizations as topics because those nominalizations refer to ideas in sentences that went before. That is an important use of nominalizations: to sum up in one phrase actions you have just mentioned so that you can comment on them.

To account for the relationships among colonies of related samples, it is necessary to track their genetic history through hundreds of generations. **This kind of study** requires a careful history of a colony.

Here is a quick way to determine how well you have managed your topics in a passage. Run a line under the first five or six words of every sentence (in fact under the subject of every verb in every clause, if you can do it). Read the phrases you underlined straight through. If any of them seems clearly outside the general set of topics, check whether it refers to ideas mentioned toward the end of the previous sentence. If not, consider revising.

Again, do not take this to mean that you have to make your topics identical or that all your topics have to be in subjects. A topic string is consistent to the degree that your reader can see connections in the sequence of words and phrases that open your sentences (and clauses). You will change your topic strings as you begin a new section or a new paragraph. The crucial point is not to force your reader to begin each sentence in a sequence of sentences with information that the reader will find startling, unfamiliar, unexpected, disconnected from any of the other topics or from the end of the immediately preceding sentence.

The best diagnosis, however, is your own sensibility. When you stuff your prose with nominalizations and passives, it feels bloated. When you jump from topic to topic, your prose will feel different—disjointed, choppy, out of focus. Be sensitive to how you feel when you read and you will develop an instinct for where to look when you don't like what you've written. You will also know where to begin revising.

Some Special Problems with Topics

Audience as Topic

From time to time, some of us have to write for an audience able to understand only the simplest prose. Or more often, we have to write on a matter so complex that even a competent reader will understand it only if we take special care to make it clear. This does not mean "dumbing down." It means only that we take special care to apply everything that we have said so far—an agent/action style, consistent topics, a predictable flow of old-new information. But we can make our prose more immediate, more available to the reader, if in those sentences we can also make the reader the topic of a sequence of sentences.

Here is some advice on renting a house that appeared in a publication directed to a broad audience:

> The following information should be verified in every lease before signing: a full description of the premises to be rented and its exact location; the amount, frequency, and dates of payments; the amounts of deposits and prepayment of rents; a statement setting forth the conditions under which the deposit will be refunded.

That's not particularly difficult for an educated reader. But we can make it clearer, more reader-friendly, if you will, if we bring the reader into the flow of information in the form of *you:*

> When you get the lease from the landlord, do not sign it right away. Before you sign, make sure the lease . . .
> (1) describes the place that you are renting;
> (2) states where it is;

(3) states
     • how much rent you have to pay
     • how often you have to pay it
     • on what day you have to pay it;
(4) states
     • how much security deposit you have to pay
     • how much rent you have to pay before you move in;
(5) states when the landlord can keep your deposit.

I did more than shorten sentences, use simple words, and put agents into subjects, and actions into verbs. I also made the reader and the reader's experience a direct part of the discourse. (I also used a tabular arrangement with lots of white space. Had it been longer, I could have broken it up with headings and subheadings.)

Even complex material will yield to this kind of revision. If, for example, you are trying to explain some complex matter of taxes, imagine explaining the problem to someone sitting across the table. Since that person has to pay the taxes, you would begin most of your sentences with *you*. As you write—or rewrite—simply make a point of beginning every sentence with *you*. If you think the prose sounds too chatty, you can always replace the *you* with some third-person subject—*the taxpayer*. Compare:

> To maximize eventual postretirement after-tax cash flow, the decision between a taxfree rollover of the imminent distribution into an IRA, or lump-sum ten-year forward averaging depends on whether the benefits of tax deferral will exceed the benefits of paying a small tax at the time of monthly distribution, though as a general rule, tax deferral will rarely exceed the benefits of a low tax rate.

> To receive the most money after taxes, you have to decide what to do with the lump sum you will receive.
> (1) You can roll it over into your IRA and then defer taxes until you start withdrawing it after you retire.
> (2) You can average it over ten years and pay taxes on it now. You will probably have more money if you roll it over because when you retire, you'll probably pay taxes at a lower rate.

It's true that if these revisions are more readable, they are also a bit longer. But we ought not assume that they are therefore less economical, at least not if we judge economy by a measure more sophisticated than counting words. The real measure of economy should be whether we have achieved our ends, whether our readers understand or do what we want them to. The next is perhaps a more telling example.

In 1985, the Government Accounting Office sponsored a study that inquired into why fewer than half the automobile owners who receive recall letters complied. It found that many car owners could not understand the letters. I received the following. It is an example of how writers can simultaneously meet legal requirements and ignore ethical obligations.

> A defect which involves the possible failure of a frame support plate may exist on your vehicle. This plate (front suspension pivot bar support plate) connects a portion of the front suspension to the vehicle frame, and its failure could affect vehicle directional control, particularly during heavy brake application. In addition, your vehicle may require adjustment service to the hood secondary catch system. The secondary catch may be misaligned so that the hood may not be adequately restrained to prevent hood fly-up in the event the primary latch is inadvertently left unengaged. Sudden hood fly-up beyond the secondary catch while driving could impair driver visibility. In certain circumstances, occurrence of either of the above conditions could result in vehicle crash without prior warning.

The author—probably a committee—nominalized all the verbs that might make a reader anxious, made most of the rest of the other verbs passive, and then deleted just about all references to the characters, particularly to the manufacturer. You might try revising this along the lines of the others. Certainly one of the sentences will read,

> If you brake hard and the plate fails, you will not be able to steer your car.

Designing Topics

A writer can create quite subtle effects by finding verbs that will let him shift into the subject/topic position those characters that will best serve his purposes. Children learn how quickly. Even four year olds understand the difference between,

> When **Tom and I** bumped, **my glass** dropped, and the **juice spilled.**

> When I bumped into Tom I dropped my glass and spilled the juice.

Neither sentence is more or less "true" to the facts. But while both have an agent-action style, the second assigns responsibility to an agent in a way different from the first.

We best appreciate this design when we recognize how skilled writers draw on the resources of English syntax to achieve important ends. Here are the first few sentences of Lincoln's Gettysburg Address, rewritten from a plausible and coherent topical point view, but rather different from Lincoln's original:

> Four score and seven years ago, **this continent** witnessed the birth of a new nation, conceived in liberty and dedicated to the proposition of our fathers that all men are created equal. Now, **this great Civil War** that engages us is testing whether **that nation or any nation** so conceived and so dedicated can long endure.
>
> **The War** created this great battlefield. **A portion of it** is now to be dedicated as the final resting place for those who here gave their lives that this nation might live. **This** is altogether a fitting and proper thing to do. But in a larger sense, **this ground** will not let us dedicate, consecrate, or hallow it. It has already taken that consecration from the brave men, living and dead, who struggled here, far above our poor power to add or detract. **Our words** will be little noted nor long remembered, but **their actions** will never pass from human memory.

Compare the original:

> Four score and seven years ago **our fathers** brought forth on this continent a new nation, conceived in liberty, and dedicated to the proposition that **all men** are created equal.
>
> Now **we** are engaged in a great civil war, testing whether **that nation,** or any nation so conceived and so dedicated, can long endure. **We** are met on a great battlefield of that war. **We** have come to dedicate a portion of that field as a final resting place for **those who** here gave their lives that **that nation** might live. It is altogether fitting and proper that **we** should do this.
>
> But, in a larger sense, **we** cannot dedicate—**we** cannot consecrate—**we** cannot hallow this ground. **The brave men,** living and dead, who struggled here have consecrated it, far above our poor power to add or detract. **The world** will little note, nor long remember that **we** say here, but it can never forget what **they** did here. It is for **us the living,** rather, to be dedicated here to the unfinished work which **they who** fought here have thus far so nobly advanced. It is rather for **us** to be here dedicated to the great task remaining before us—that from these honored dead **we** take increased devotion to that cause for which **they** gave the last full

measure of devotion—that **we** here highly resolve that **these dead** shall not have died in vain—that **this nation,** under God, shall have a new birth of freedom—and that **government of the people, by the people, and for the people,** shall not perish from the earth.

Lincoln assigned responsibility to his audience. By consistently topicalizing *we* to make himself and his audience the agents of the crucial actions, Lincoln made them one with the founding fathers and with the men who fought and died at Gettysburg. By so doing, he tacitly invited his listeners to join their dead forefathers and their dead countrymen in making the great sacrifices the living had still to make to preserve the Union.

My revision shifts agency away from people and assigns it to abstractions and places: *the continent witnesses, a great civil war tests, the war creates, the ground will not let, it has taken.* I have metaphorically invested agency and responsibility not in people but in abstractions. Had Lincoln presented my version, he would have relieved his audience of their responsibility to act, and would thereby have deprived us of one of the great documents in our history.

You may think at this point that I am saying it is always good to design prose so that agents always act on their own responsibility; that when we deflect responsibility away from people, when we topicalize abstractions, we create prose that is less honest, less direct than prose whose agents act as topic/subjects. Not so. If in 1775 Thomas Jefferson had followed that advice, he would have written a very different Declaration of Independence. Note in the first two paragraphs of the original how Jefferson seems to have *designed* most of the sentences so that they do not open with the colonists acting as agents, asserting their own actions, but rather with words that topicalize mostly events, rights, duties, needs—concepts that make the colonists the objects of more actions than they initiate, concepts that force colonists to act on behalf of higher forces (I boldface what seem to be main topics of clauses and italicize actions):

> **When in the Course of human events,** it *becomes necessary* for one people to dissolve the political bands which have connected them with another, and to assume among the powers of the earth, the separate and equal station to which the Laws of Nature and of Nature's God entitle them, **a decent respect to the opinions of mankind** *requires* that they should declare the causes which impel them to the separation.

We *hold* these truths to be self-evident, that **all men** *are cre-ated equal,* that **they** *are endowed* by their Creator with certain unalienable Rights, that among **these** *are Life, Liberty and the pursuit of Happiness.* That to secure these rights, **Governments** *are instituted* among Men, deriving their just powers from the consent of the governed. That whenever **any Form of Government** *becomes destructive* of these ends, it is **the Right of the People** *to alter or to abolish* it, and to institute new Government, laying its foundation on such principles and organizing its powers in such form, as to them shall seem most likely to affect their Safety and Happiness. **Prudence,** indeed, *will dictate* that **Governments long established** *should not be changed* for light and transient causes. . . .

Contrast that opening with a version in which the colonists are the consistent and freely acting topic/agents of every action:

When **we** *decided* that **we** *would dissolve* the political bands that connected us with Britain and that **we** *would assume* among the powers of the earth the separate and equal station that **we** *claim* through the Laws of Nature and of Nature's God, then since **we** decently *respect* the opinions of mankind, **we** *decided* that **we** *would declare* why **we** *do* so. **These truths** *are* self-evident—**we** *are all equal* in our creation, **we** *derive* from God certain Rights that **we** *intend to keep,* **and among those rights, we** *include* Life, Liberty and the opportunity to make ourselves Happy. [Try revising the rest of the passage along the same lines.]

In my version, I have topicalized the revolutionary colonists, making them the main players, acting simply because they will themselves to act. Jefferson topicalized abstractions, subordinat-ing the will of the revolutionaries to a higher force that acts on them. But after Jefferson established the principles that forced the colonists to act by animating and topicalizing a higher neces-sity, he switched his topic/subjects to King George, an agent whom Jefferson made seem to act entirely out of malign will:

He *has refused* his Assent to Laws, the most wholesome and necessary for the public good.

He *has forbidden* his Governors to pass Laws of immediate and pressing importance, unless suspended in their operation till his Assent should be obtained; and when so suspended, **he** *has utterly neglected* to attend to them.

He *has refused* to pass other Laws for the accommodation of large districts of people, unless those people would relinquish the

right of Representation in the Legislature, a right inestimable to
them and formidable to tyrants only.
　　He *has called* together. . . .
　　He *has dissolved* Representative Houses. . . .
　　. . . . .
　　He *has excited* domestic insurrections. . . .

Someone who believed in the divine right of kings could have
made George the constrained object of demands from some
Higher Order:

> **Duty to His Divine responsibilities** *demanded* that **Assent to Laws**
> not issue from his office. . . . **Prudence** *required* His opposition to
> Laws for the accommodation of large districts of people. . . . *It*
> *was necessary* to call together . . . **The dissolution of Represen-**
> **tative Houses** *became needful* when . . .

When he was finished with this bill of particulars, Jefferson
was ready to move to his third set of subjects/topics/agents and
draw the inevitable conclusion (the capitalization in the last
paragraph is Jefferson's):

> In every stage of these Oppressions **We** have Petitioned for Re-
> dress in the most humble terms: **Our repeated Petitions** have been
> answered only by repeated injury. **A Prince,** whose character is
> thus marked by every act which may define a Tyrant, is unfit to be
> the ruler of a free people.
>
> Nor have **We** been wanting in attention to our British breth-
> ren. **We** have warned them from time to time of attempts by their
> legislature to extend an unwarrantable jurisdiction over us. **We**
> have reminded them of the circumstances of our emigration and
> settlement here. **We** have appealed to their native justice and mag-
> nanimity, and **we** have conjured them by the ties of our common
> kindred to disavow these usurpations, which would inevitably in-
> terrupt our connections and correspondence. **They** too have been
> deaf to the voice of justice and of consanguinity. **We** must, there-
> fore, acquiesce in the necessity, which denounces our Separation,
> and hold them, as **we** hold the rest of mankind, Enemies in War,
> in Peace Friends.
>
> **We,** THEREFORE, the Representatives of the UNITED STATES OF
> AMERICA, in General Congress, Assembled, appealing to the Su-
> preme Judge of the world for the rectitude of our intentions, do,
> in the Name, and by Authority of the good People of these Colo-
> nies, solemnly publish and declare, That **these United Colonies**
> are, and of Right ought to be FREE AND INDEPENDENT STATES;

that **they** are Absolved from all Allegiance to the British Crown, and that **all political connection between them and the State of Great Britain,** is and ought to be totally dissolved; and that as **Free and Independent States, they** have full Power to levy War, conclude Peace, contract Alliances, establish Commerce, and to do all other Acts and Things which Independent States may of right do. And for the support of this Declaration, with a firm reliance on the protection of Divine Providence, **we** mutually pledge to each other our Lives, our Fortunes and our sacred Honor.

Did Jefferson "intend" to create this systematic sequence of topic/subject/agents, beginning with abstractions, moving to *he,* and concluding with *we?* We can no more answer that question than we can know what any great writer intends. But once a coherent pattern emerges, we have to treat that pattern as part of a design in the service of some larger end.

The lesson to be drawn here (both politically and stylistically, perhaps) is that all local principles must yield to higher principles. The real problem is to recognize those occasions when we should subordinate one principle to another. That's not something I can help you with. That knowledge comes only with experience.

Summing Up

1. Generally, use the beginning of your sentences to refer to what you have already mentioned or knowledge that you can assume you and your reader readily share. Compare these:

> The huge number of wounded and dead in **the Civil War** exceeded all the **other wars in American history.** One of the reasons for the lingering animosity between North and South today is **the memory of this terrible carnage.**

> Of **all the wars in American history,** none has exceeded **the Civil War** in the huge number of wounded and dead. **The memory of this terrible carnage** is one of the reasons for the animosity between North and South today.

2. Choose topics that will control your reader's point of view. This will depend on how creatively you can use verbs to make one or another of your characters the seeming agent of an action. Which of these would better serve the needs of a patient suing a physician is obvious:

A patient whose reactions go unmonitored may also claim physician liability. In this case, a patient took Cloromax as prescribed, which resulted in partial renal failure. The manufacturer's literature indicated that the patient should be observed frequently and should immediately report any sign of infection. Evidence indicated that the patient had not received instructions to report any signs of urinary blockage. Moreover, the patient had no white cell count taken until after he developed the blockage.

If a physician does not monitor his patient's reactions, he may be held liable. In this case, the physician prescribed Cloromax, which caused the patient to experience partial renal failure. The physician had been cautioned by the manufacturer's literature that he should observe the patient frequently and instruct the patient to report any sign of infection. Evidence indicates that the physician also failed to instruct the patient to report any sign of urinary blockage. Moreover, he failed to take any white cell count until after the patient developed the blockage.

We can integrate the general guiding principles—not binding rules—in this:

FIXED	TOPIC	
VARIABLE	OLD INFORMATION	NEW INFORMATION

FIXED	SUBJECT	VERB	COMPLEMENT
VARIABLE	CHARACTERS	ACTION	

Organize your sentences so that you open them with old information in the topic position, usually with a character as a subject. Then follow the subject with a verb that expresses a crucial action. Move complex information to the end of your sentence. Then be certain that your string of topics is consistent and appropriate. At this point, your good judgment has to take control.

All's well that ends well.
William Shakespeare

In the end is my beginning.
T. S. Eliot

4

Emphasis

If you begin a sentence well, the end will almost take care of itself. So the first step toward a style that is clear, direct, and coherent lies in how you manage the first few words of every sentence. If at the beginning of your sentences, you consistently organize your subject/topics around a few central characters or concepts and then move quickly to close that subject with a precise verb expressing a crucial action, then by default you will have to put important new information at the ends of your sentences. If you do not manage the flow of your ideas in this way, your prose will seem not just unfocused, but weak, anticlimactic. Compare these two sentences:

> A charge of gross violation of academic responsibility is required for a Board of Trustees to dismiss a tenured faculty member for cause, and an elaborate hearing procedure with a prior statement of charges is provided for before a tenured faculty member may be dismissed for cause, in most States.

> In most States, before a Board of Trustees may dismiss a tenured faculty member for cause, it must charge him with a gross violation of academic responsibility and provide him with a statement of charges and an elaborate hearing procedure.

The first trails off; the second builds a climactic rhythm.

Because one element that opens a sentence is so important, we named it *topic*. Since the end of a sentence plays a role no less crucial, we should give it a name as well. When you utter a sentence, your voice naturally rises and falls. When you approach the end, you ordinarily raise your pitch on one of those last few words and stress it a bit more strongly than you do the others:

o
. . . a bit more strongly than the

thers.

This rising pitch and stress signal the end of a sentence. We'll call that part of a sentence its *stress*.

Managing Endings

We manage the information in this stressed part of the sentence in several ways. We can put our most important information there in the first place. More often, we have to revise our sentences to give the right information the right emphasis.

Trim the end. In some cases, we can just lop off final unnecessary words until we get to the information we want to stress, leaving that information in the final stressed position.

> Sociobiologists are making the provocative claim that our genes largely determine our social behavior in the way we act in situations we find around us every day.

Since *social behavior* means the way we act, we can just drop everything after *behavior:*

> Sociobiologists are making the provocative claim that our genes largely determine our social behavior.

Shift less important information to the left. One way to revise for emphasis is to move unimportant phrases away from the end of a sentence to expose what you want to emphasize:

> The data that are offered to establish the existence of ESP do not make believers of us **for the most part.**

> **For the most part,** the data that are offered to establish the existence of ESP do not make us believers.

Occasionally, when we shift a phrase, we may have to separate subjects from verbs or verbs from objects. This sentence ends weakly:

> No one can explain why that first primeval superatom exploded and thereby created the universe in a few words.

The modifier of *explain (in a few words)* is much shorter than the object of *explain* (the clause *why that first primeval super-*

atom exploded and thereby created the universe). To create better emphasis, we put that short, less important modifier before the longer, more important object, even if we have to split the object from its verb:

> No one can explain **in a few words** why that first primeval superatom exploded and thereby created the universe.

Shift important information to the right. Moving the important information to the end of a sentence is another way to manage the flow of ideas. And the sentence you just read illustrates a missed opportunity. This is more cohesive and emphatic:

> Another way you can manage the flow of ideas is to move the most important information to the end of the sentence.

In fact, this is just the other side of something we've already seen—how to move old information to the beginning of a sentence. Sentences that introduce a paragraph or a new section are frequently of an *X is Y* form. One part, usually older information, glances back at what has gone before; the other announces something new. As we have seen, the older information should come first, the newer last. When it doesn't, we can often reverse the order of subjects and what follows the verb:

> Those questions relating to the ideal system for providing instruction in home computers are **just as confused.**

> **Just as confused** are those questions relating to the ideal system for providing instruction in home computers.

The switch not only puts the reference to the preceding sentences, *Just as confused,* early, but it also puts at the end information that the next several sentences will probably address.

> . . . instruction in home computers. For example, should the instruction be connected to some source of information, or. . . .

Sometimes, you can move a relative clause out of the subject:

> A discovery **that will change the course of world history and the very foundations of our understanding of ourselves and our place in the scheme of things** is imminent.

> A discovery is imminent **that will change the course of world history and the very foundations of our understanding of ourselves and our place in the scheme of things.**

Don't shift the clause if it creates an ambiguous construction. In this sentence, the clause seems to modify *staff*:

> A marketing approach has been developed by the staff **that will provide us with a new way of looking at our current problems.**

Extract and isolate. When you put your most important ideas in the middle of a long sentence, the sentence will swallow them up. A way to recover the appropriate emphasis is to break the sentence in two, either just before or just after that important idea. Then revise the new sentences so that you guide your reader to the crucial information. That often means you have to isolate the point of a long sentence by putting it into a shorter sentence of its own.

> Under the Clean Water Act, the EPA will promulgate new standards for the treatment of industrial wastewater prior to its discharge into sewers leading to publicly owned treatment plants, with pretreatment standards for types of industrial sources being discretionary, depending on local conditions, instead of imposing nationally uniform standards now required under the Act.

First, break up the sentence:

> Under the Clean Water Act, the EPA will promulgate new standards for the treatment of industrial wastewater prior to its discharge into sewers that lead to publicly owned treatment plants. Standards for types of industrial sources will be discretionary. They will depend on local conditions, instead of imposing the nationally uniform standards now required under the act.

Then rearrange to get the right emphasis:

> Under the Clean Water Act, the EPA will promulgate new standards for the treatment of industrial wastewater before it is discharged into sewers leading to publicly owned treatment plants. Unlike the standards now required under the act, the new standards will not be uniform across the whole nation. They instead will be discretionary, depending on local conditions.

The point here is the discretionary nature of the rules and their dependence on local conditions—two ideas that the next sentences will probably expand on. So we express that point in its own sentence and put it at the end, in the stress position.

When we ignore these principles of old and new information,

we risk writing prose that is both confusing and weak. Read these next few sentences aloud. Hear how your voice trails off into a lower note when, at the ends of the sentences, you have to repeat words that you read earlier, such as *infringe on patents.* Then listen to how the rewritten version lifts your voice up and brings it down emphatically on the words that ought to be stressed.

> In 1972, the United States Supreme Court declared that components of a patented assembly could be produced in this country without infringing on US patents. Since then, several cases have tested whether various combinations of imported and domestic items could be produced without infringing on US patents. The courts have consistently held any combination would infringe. However, the concept of local production and foreign assembly has not been tested as to infringement.

> In 1972, the United States Supreme Court declared that components of a patented assembly could be produced in this country without infringing on US patents. Since then, this concept has been tested by several cases involving various combinations of imported and domestic items. The courts have consistently held that US patents would be infringed by any combination. What has not been tested, however, is the concept of local production and foreign assembly.

Some Syntactic Devices

There are a few grammatical patterns that add weight to the end of a sentence.

There. I wrote the sentence above without realizing that I had illustrated this first pattern. I could have written,

> A few grammatical patterns add weight to the end of a sentence.

If you begin too many sentences with "There is" or "There are," your prose will become flat-footed, lacking movement or energy. But you can open a sentence with *there* in order to push to the end of that sentence those ideas that the next sentences will build on. In other words, like the first sentence of this section, a *there-* sentence lets you introduce in its stress the topics for the following string of sentences. Again, you may remember someone telling you not to begin sentences with *there*. More bad advice. Like passives, *there-* constructions have a function: to stress those ideas that you intend to develop in following sentences.

What. A *what-* sentence throws special emphasis on what follows a linking verb. Compare the emphasis of:

> This country needs a monetary policy that will end the violent fluctuations in money supply, unemployment, and inflation.

> **What** this country **is** a monetary policy that will end the violent fluctuations in money supply, unemployment, and inflation.

You have to pay for this added emphasis with a few more words, so use the pattern sparingly.

It- shift 1. By using *it* as a fill-in subject, you can shift a long introductory clause that would otherwise have been the subject to a position after the verb:

> **That domestic oil prices must eventually rise to the level set by OPEC** once seemed inevitable.

> It once seemed inevitable **that domestic oil prices must eventually rise to the level set by OPEC.**

It- shift 2. With this pattern, you simultaneously select and emphasize a topic and throw added weight on the stress. Compare:

> In 1933 this country experienced a depression that almost wrecked our democratic system of government.

> **It was in 1933** that this country experienced a depression that almost wrecked our democratic system of government.

Because all these syntactic patterns are so self-conscious, and because a few of them actually obscure topics, use them sparingly.

When All Else Fails

If you find yourself stuck with a sentence that ends flatly because you have to repeat a phrase you used in a previous sentence, at least try changing the phrase to a pronoun:

> When the rate of inflation dropped in 1983, large numbers of investors fled the bond market and invested in **stocks.** However,

those particularly interested in the high tech market often did not carefully investigate **the stocks.**

When the rate of inflation dropped in 1983, large numbers of investors fled the bond market and invested in **stocks.** However, those particularly interested in the high tech market often did not carefully investigate **them.**

By substituting the pronoun for the lightly stressed repeated word, you throw the emphasis on the word before the pronoun.

Finally, avoid ending a sentence with metadiscourse. Nothing ends a sentence more anticlimactically, as we see:

The opportunities we offer are particularly rich at the graduate level, **it must be remembered.**

The opportunities we offer are, **it must be remembered,** particularly rich at the graduate level.

Nuances of Emphasis

When we write highly technical prose, we often write to an audience that understands as well as we do—or better—the complex terminology, the background, the habits of mind that workers in that field have to control. When we do, we don't have to explain technical terms as we would to a layperson.

But the problem in writing for a nonexpert audience is more complex than merely defining strange terms. If for a nonexpert audience I used terms like *sarcomere, tropomyosin,* and *myoplasm,* I would not only have to define them; I would also have to take care to locate those words at that point where my reader is most ready to receive them—at the end of a sentence.

In these next two passages, underline each term that you do not understand. Once you have underlined the occurrence of a term, don't underline it again in that passage. (As you read the second passage, assume you are reading it for the first time.) Then generalize: Where in the two passages do the technical terms typically occur? How does that difference affect how easily you can read the two versions? What other devices did I use to revise the first into the second? One sentence in the second still has all the characteristics of prose written for an insider: which one?

An understanding of the activation of muscle groups depends on an appreciation of the effects of calcium blockers. The proteins

actin, myosin, tropomyosin, and troponin make up the sarcomere, the basic unit of muscle contraction. Its thick filament is
composed of myosin, which is an ATPase or energy-producing
protein. Actin, tropomyosin, and troponin make up its thin filament. There is a close association between the regulatory proteins, tropomyosin and troponin, and the contractile protein,
actin, in the thin filament. The interaction of actin and myosin is
controlled by tropomyosin. Troponin I, which participates in the
interaction between actin and myosin; troponin T, which binds
troponin to tropomyosin; and troponin C, which binds calcium
constitute three peptide chains of troponin. An excess of 10^{-7} for
the myoplasmic concentration of Ca^{++} leads to its binding to troponin C. The inhibitory forces of tropomyosin are removed, and
the complex interaction of actin and myosin is manifested as
contraction.

To contract, muscles use calcium. When we understand what
calcium does, we understand how muscles are affected by calcium
blocker drugs.

The fundamental unit of muscle contraction is the sarcomere.
The sarcomere has two filaments, one thin and one thick. These
filaments are composed of proteins that cause and prevent contraction. Two of these proteins cause a muscle to contract. One is
in the thin filament—the protein actin. The other protein is in the
thick filament—myosin, an energy producing or ATPase protein.
When actin in the thin filament interacts with myosin in the thick
filament, the muscle contracts.

The thin filament also has proteins that inhibit contraction.
They are the proteins troponin and tropomyosin. Troponin has
three peptide chains: troponin I, troponin T, and troponin C.

 (a) troponin I participates in the interaction between actin
      and myosin;
 (b) troponin T binds troponin to tropomyosin;
 (c) troponin C binds calcium.

When a muscle is relaxed, tropomyosin in the thin filament inhibits actin, also in the thin filament, from interacting with the
myosin in the thick filament. But when the concentration of Ca^{++}
in the myoplasm in the sarcomere exceeds 10^{-7}, the calcium binds
to troponin C. The tropomyosin then no longer inhibits actin and
myosin from interacting and the muscle contracts.

For the novice in muscle chemistry, the second version is more
readable than the first. Yet both have the same technical terms. In
fact, the second has no more information than the first. The versions differ, however, in two ways.

1. In the second, I made explicit some of the information that the first only implied—the sarcomere has thick and thin filaments—or information that was indirectly stated in an adjective—converting *regulatory protein* into *proteins that regulate*.

2. In the second, I introduced technical terms at the ends of their sentences.

So in addition to everything we learned in Chapters 2 and 3, here is another key to communicating complex information that requires terminology unfamiliar to your readers: when you introduce a technical term for the first time—or even a familiar but very important term—design the sentence it appears in so that you can locate that term at the end, in its stress, *never at the beginning, in its topic,* even if you have to invent a sentence simply for the sake of defining or emphasizing that term.

Writers often introduce terms in this same way even in highly technical writing for a relatively specialized audience. This passage is from an article in *The New England Journal of Medicine* (note as well the metadiscourse *we*):

> We have previously described a method for generating lymphocytes with antitumor reactivity. The incubation of peripheral-blood lymphocytes with a lymphokine, interleukin-2, generates lymphoid cells that can lyse fresh, noncultured, natural-killer-cell-resistant tumor cells but not normal cells. **We have termed these cells lymphokine-activated killer (LAK) cells.**

Compare these two passages. One of them was written by W. Averell Harriman for an article in the *New York Times.*

> The Administration has blurred the issue of verification—so central to arms control. Irresponsible charges, innuendo and leaks have submerged serious problems with Soviet compliance. The objective, instead, should be not to exploit these concerns in order to further poison our relations, repudiate existing agreements, or, worse still, terminate arms control altogether, but to clarify questionable Soviet behavior and insist on compliance.

> The issue of verification—so central to arms control—has been blurred by the Administration. Serious problems with Soviet compliance have been submerged in irresponsible charges, innuendo and leaks. The objective, instead, should be to clarify questionable Soviet behavior and insist on compliance—not to exploit these concerns in order to further poison our relations, repudiate existing agreements, or, worse still, terminate arms control altogether.

In the original article, Harriman was attacking what he believed were the President's misguided policies. Look at the way the sentences in the two versions end, at what each stresses. As you have probably guessed, Harriman's version is the second one, the one that stresses *blurred by the Administration, irresponsible charges, innuendo and leaks, poison our relations . . . terminate arms control altogether.* It is this second version in which Harriman comes down hard not on references to the Soviet Union, but on references to a Republican administration.

In some cases, a writer can manipulate the stress of sentences in ways that encourage us to respond not to what *is* new, but to what we should *take* as new, what we should take as familiar. In this next passage, Joan Didion arranged what should be unsurprising and familiar, new and shocking in a way that seems to contradict our principles. Look at how she ends her sentences at the point where she begins to describe the dark side of Los Angeles (they are boldfaced):

We put "Lay Lady Lay" on the record player, and "Suzanne." We went down to Melrose Avenue to see the Flying Burritos. There was a jasmine vine grown over the verandah of the big house on Franklin Avenue, and in the evenings the smell of jasmine came in through all the open doors and windows. I made bouillabaisse for people who did not eat meat. I imagined that my own life was simple and sweet, and sometimes it was, but there were odd things **going on around town.** There were **rumors.** There were **stories.** Everything was unmentionable but nothing was **unimaginable.** This mystical flirtation with the idea of "sin"— this sense that it was possible to go "too far," and that many people were doing it—was very much **with us in Los Angeles in 1968 and 1969.** A demented and seductive vortical tension was building **in the community.** The jitters were **setting in.** I recall a time when the dogs barked every night and the moon was **always full.** On August 9, 1969, I was sitting in the shallow end of my sister-in-law's swimming pool in Beverly Hills when she received a telephone call from a friend who had just heard about the murders **at Sharon Tate Polanski's house on Cielo Drive.** The phone rang many times **during the next hour.** These early reports were **garbled** and **contradictory.** One caller would say **hoods,** the next would say **chains.** There were twenty dead, no twelve, ten, **eighteen.** Black masses were imagined and bad trips **blamed.** I remember all of the day's misinformation very **clearly,** and I also

remember this, and I wish I did not: *I remember that **no one was surprised.***
—Joan Didion, "The White Album"[7]

Read just the bold-faced words and phrases—with the exception of *hoods* and *chains*, they convey largely mundane information. We might expect an ordinary writer to locate at the ends of her sentences information that would shock and surprise us. But Didion is writing about the very lack of surprise, that what in ordinary times would be shocking did not surprise her circle because evil was somehow already familiar. To reflect just that sense of eerie familiarity, she constructs her sentences to locate her references to evil in the least emphatic places. What is unexpected is only where the evil emerged and how.

Here is that passage revised according to our principles, a revision that is substantially less interesting than the original.

> The record player played "Lay Lady Lay" and "Suzanne." We went down to Melrose Avenue to see the Flying Burritos. At the big house on Franklin Avenue there was a jasmine vine grown over the verandah and in the evenings the smell of jasmine came in through all the open doors and windows. I made bouillabaisse for people who did not eat meat. I imagined that my own life was simple and sweet, and sometimes it was, but going around town were some things that seemed **odd**. There were **stories**. There were **rumors**. Everything was unmentionable but nothing was **unimaginable**. In Los Angeles in 1968 and 1969, we all had this sense that it was possible to go "too far," and that many people were **doing it**. It was a mystical flirtation with the idea of "**sin**." Our community was building a vortical tension, a tension that was **seductive and demented**. We were getting **the jitters**. I recall a time when the dogs barked every night and the moon was **always full**. On August 9, 1969, as I was sitting in the shallow end of my sister-in-law's swimming pool in Beverly Hills, she received a telephone call from a friend who had just heard that over on Cielo drive, at Roman Polanski's house, Sharon Tate and others **had been murdered**. During the next hour the phone **rang many times**. These early reports were **garbled and contradictory**. One caller would say **hoods**, the next would say **chains**. There were ten, no twelve, eighteen, **twenty dead**. People blamed bad trips and imagined **black masses**. I remember very clearly all of the day's **misinformation**, and I also remember this, and I wish I did not: *I remember that it surprised **no one**.*

The System of Clarity

By now, we begin to appreciate the extraordinary complexity of an ordinary English sentence. A sentence is more than its subject, verb, and object. It is more than the sum of its words and parts. It is a system of systems whose parts we can fit together in very delicate ways to achieve very delicate ends—if we know how. We can match, mismatch, or metaphorically manipulate the grammatical units and their meanings:

SUBJECT	VERB	COMPLEMENT
CHARACTERS	ACTION	—

We can match or mismatch rhetorical units to create more or less important meanings:

TOPIC	STRESS
OLD/LESS IMPORTANT	NEW/MORE IMPORTANT

And we can fit these two systems into a larger system:

TOPIC		STRESS	
OLD/LESS IMPORTANT		NEW/MORE IMPORTANT	
SUBJECT	VERB	COMPLEMENT	
CHARACTERS	ACTION	—	

Of course, we don't want every one of our sentences to march lockstep across the page in a rigid character-action order. When a writer exercises his stylistic imagination in the way Jefferson did with the Declaration of Independence, he can create and control fine shades of agency, action, emphasis, and point of view. But if for no good reason he writes sentences that consistently depart from any coherent pattern, if he consistently hides agency, nominalizes active verbs into passive nominalizations, and if he consistently ends sentences on secondary information, he will write prose that is not just turgid, but incoherent.

In fact, when we stand back from the details of subjects, agents, passives, nominalizations, topic and stress, when we listen to our prose, we should hear something beyond sheer clarity and coherence. We should hear a voice. The voice our readers hear contributes substantially to the character we project—or more accurately, to the character our readers construct.

Some teachers of writing want to make voice a moral choice between a false voice and the voice "authentic." I suspect that we all speak in many voices, no one of which is more or less false, more or less authentic than any other. When you want to be pompous and authoritative, then that's in the voice you project because that's what you are being. When you want to be laconic and direct, then you should be able to adopt that voice. The problem is to hear the voice you are projecting and to change it when you want to. That's no more false than choosing how you dress, how you behave, how you live.

Form is not something added to substance as a mere protruberant adornment. The two are fused into a unity. . . . The strength that is born of form and the feebleness that is born of lack of form are in truth qualities of substance. They are the tokens of the thing's identity. They make it what it is.
Benjamin Cardozo

Style and structure are the essence of a book; great ideas are hogwash.
Vladimir Nabokov

I always write a good first line, but I have trouble in writing the others.
Molière

Let it not be said that I have said nothing new. The arrangement of the material is new.
Blaise Pascal

5

Coherence I

Form Beyond Sentences

All of us have stopped in the middle of a memo, an article, or a book realizing that while we may have understood its words and sentences, we don't quite know what they should all add up to. In this chapter and the next, we will offer some principles that will help you diagnose that kind of writing and then revise it. We will illustrate these principles mostly with paragraphs, but we can generalize from paragraphs to sections of documents, even to whole documents, because the principles that make paragraphs coherent apply to prose of any length. Like our other principles, they are principles of reading that we have translated into principles of writing. No one or two of them is sufficient to make a reader feel a passage is coherent. They are a set of principles that writers have to orchestrate toward that common end.

Some cautions: some of the vocabulary in this chapter will be unfamiliar. We dislike jargon as intensely as anyone, but we have had to create terms for new concepts about coherence that we think writers must understand. These principles are also more abstract than those about subjects and characters, about nominalizations and verbs, because coherence is abstract; we cannot point to it as we can point to a noun. Finally, we do not offer these principles as rules that dictate the creation of every paragraph. They are diagnostic tools to help you anticipate when your readers may think your writing is incoherent and to suggest how you can revise it.

You have already seen the first principle.

Principle 1: A cohesive paragraph has consistent topic strings.

There are four more:

Principle 2: A cohesive paragraph has another set of strings running through it that we will call *thematic strings*.

Principle 3: A cohesive paragraph introduces new topic and thematic strings in a predictable location: at the end of
the sentence(s) that introduce the paragraph.

Principle 4: A coherent paragraph will usually have a single sentence that clearly articulates its point.

Principle 5: A coherent paragraph will typically locate that point
sentence in one of two places.

We cover the first three principles in this chapter, the last two in
the next.

What's All This About? Topic Strings Again, Briefly

Principle 1: Readers will feel that a paragraph is cohesive if it has
consistent topic strings.

In Chapter 3, we explained how two principles of reading
shape a reader's point of view:

1. Readers need familiar information at the beginnings of sentences.

2. Readers will take the main characters of the story as the most
consistently familiar pieces of information.

These two principles should encourage us to use the sequence of
topics—usually subjects—to focus the reader's attention on a
limited set of referents, usually characters, but also central repeated concepts. By consistent topics, we do not mean identical.
The topics should constitute a sequence that makes consistent
sense to the reader.

But since stories always have more than one character, and
since we can make abstractions act like characters, we always
have to choose our topics, to design topic strings that focus the
reader's attention on a particular point of view. In this next paragraph, the stress of the first sentence introduces evolution, a concept that the writer directly or indirectly topicalized thereafter:

Clark's practice of carefully mapping every fossil made it possible
to follow the evolutionary development of various types through
time. Beautiful sequences of antelopes, giraffes and elephants were
obtained; new species evolving out of old and appearing in younger
strata. In short, evolution was taking place before the eyes of the

Omo surveyors, and they could time it. The finest examples of this process were in several lines of pigs which had been common at Omo and had developed rapidly. Unsnarling the pig story was turned over to paleontologist Basil Cooke. He produced family trees for pigs whose various types were so accurately dated that pigs themselves became measuring sticks that could be applied to fossils of questionable age in other places that had similar pigs.
—Donald C. Johanson and Maitland A. Edey, *Lucy: The Beginnings of Humankind*[8]

The authors could have consistently topicalized the flesh-and-blood-characters:

> **Clark** obtained. . . . **The Omo surveyors** could watch. . . . And **they** could time. . . . **They** found fine examples in. . . .

We cannot follow any mechanical rule about what to topicalize. We have to decide on a point of view toward our material, consider what our readers will take to be old and new information, then design sentences to meet both needs.

But there is a second sense of "aboutness" that readers also look for.

What About the Topics? A Second Kind of String

> Principle 2: A reader will feel that a paragraph is cohesive if it has other strings of related words, strings that we will call *thematic strings*.

Read this paragraph:

> Truman had many issues to factor into his decision about the Oppenheimer committee's scientific recommendation to stop the hydrogen bomb project. A Sino-Soviet bloc had been proclaimed; the Cold War was developing; Republican leaders were withdrawing support for his foreign policy; and opinion was coming down on the side of a strong response to the first Russian atom bomb test. As a Democratic President, Truman concluded that being second in developing the hydrogen bomb was an alternative he could not risk. In retrospect, some now believe that the risk was worth taking, but they did not have to consider the issues that Truman did.

Now do a little experiment with your memory. Don't look back; it's important to determine only what you can recall. Make two lists. In one, list the characters you remember. In the other, list just two or three words that would capture the central concepts that the writer weaves around those characters, words that constitute the conceptual center of that paragraph. Do it now.

Now do the same thing with the evolution paragraph that you read earlier. Again, don't look back; write down only what you remember: central characters and two or three central concepts.

If you are like most readers, you were able to recall more key words, *conceptual* words, from the evolution paragraph than from the Truman paragraph. The writers of the evolution paragraph created a consistent topic string consisting of references to evolution and to a few characters. But they also wove through that paragraph other sets of related words:

(1) types of fossils (curly brackets): fossil, antelopes, giraffes, pigs;
(2) actions of the surveyors (small capitals): map, follow, time, etc.;
(3) actions of species (boldfaced): evolve, appear, die, replaced, etc.;
(4) time (italics): time, new, old, younger, age, etc.

> Clark's PRACTICE OF CAREFULLY MAPPING every {fossil} made it possible to FOLLOW the evolutionary **development** of various types through *time*. Beautiful **sequences** of {antelopes, giraffes and elephants} were OBTAINED; {*new* species} **evolving** out of *old* and **appearing** in *younger* strata. In short, evolution was taking place before the eyes of the Omo surveyors, and they could *time* it. The finest examples of the process were in several {lines of pigs} which **had been common** at Omo and had **developed** rapidly. UNSNARLING the {pig} story WAS TURNED OVER to paleontologist Basil Cooke. He PRODUCED family trees for {pigs} whose {various types} WERE SO ACCURATELY *dated* that {pigs} themselves became measuring sticks that COULD BE APPLIED to {fossils} of questionable *age* in other places that had {similar pigs}.

Note that these sequences of words are not just repeated words. They are sets of conceptually related words. The Truman paragraph, on the other hand, has no such network of related words.

We will call these sets of conceptually related words *themes* and sequences of them that run through a paragraph *thematic strings*. In any paragraph, the words in the topic strings and the words in thematic strings are not mutually exclusive. Some words in a topic string may turn up outside the topic position, and some words in the thematic string may turn up as topics.

Together, topic strings and thematic strings constitute the conceptual architecture of a passage, the frame within which you develop new ideas. Topic strings focus your reader's attention on what a passage is globally about. The thematic strings give your reader a sense that you are focusing on a core of ideas related to those topics.

Compare the original Truman paragraph with this one:

> When the Oppenheimer committee advised President Truman to stop the hydrogen bomb project, Truman had to consider not just scientific issues, but also how developing tensions between the U.S. and the USSR were influencing domestic politics. When the Russians and Chinese proclaimed a hostile Sino-Soviet bloc, the Cold War became a political issue. At the same time, Truman was losing Republican support for his foreign policy. So when Russia set off its first atomic bomb, Americans demanded that their President respond strongly. He decided that he could not risk voters' seeing him as letting the Russians be first in developing the most powerful weapon yet. Some critics now believe that he should have taken that risk, but they did not have to worry about Cold War American politics.

We have done more than make this paragraph more specific. We have revised it around explicit thematic words that focus the reader's attention on two central themes: first on international tension—*developing tensions between the U.S. and the USSR, a hostile Sino-Soviet bloc, the Cold War;* and then on domestic politics—*domestic politics, Republican support, voters, Cold War American politics.*

But now here is a complicating factor: readers familiar with the history of that period would not have needed those words to make the original paragraph hang together: they would have supplied their own, as some of you may have done. Those who know a great deal about a subject can create much of their own cohesion and coherence in a text on that subject because they can read into it relationships that others less knowledgeable cannot. Those who know little need all the help they can get. The problem is to understand what your reader knows about your subject. Since we ordinarily write for readers who know much less than we do about a subject, it is always prudent to underestimate a reader's knowledge and make themes explicit.

How Do Thematic Strings Go Wrong?

Too Few Strings. A paragraph that feels empty of meaning will have one or two topics, much repetition, and no specifically articulated central themes that the reader can seize on as a conceptual center for the paragraph. But once diagnosed, this problem won't yield to advice about style and organization. The writer has to think harder.

Diffuse Strings. A reader may feel a passage is unfocused if a theme is only implicit or if the writer uses no single word to pull together concepts that may seem to a reader wholly unrelated. That was the problem with the original Truman paragraph. A different form of that problem is illustrated by this next paragraph:

> Rule structuring supports cognition, whether the information comes from direct practice, witnessed demonstrations, or from symbolic modeling. Under what conditions is one social learning technique favored over another? Example can teach better than precept. This is most likely to be the case if the learners' language skills are not adequate for utilizing information cast in language symbols, or if the patterns cannot be easily captured in words. In many cases, such as in learning to ride a bicycle, verbal directions may be too cumbersome, since quick and intricate coordinations must be made. In mastering certain concepts, diverse subroutines must be integrated serially. If the content is difficult and unfamiliar, lengthy lecture presentations can tax comprehension and satiate the discerning attention of the learner. In these case, demonstration offers advantages over undiluted narration. However, if verbal symbols can be easily stored and adeptly translated into their action referents, symbolic modeling should be much more efficient than enacting actual illustration for observers.

The writer of this paragraph wanted to contrast two kinds of teaching: explanation and demonstration. But he used so many different terms to describe them that he seems to describe a dozen ways. He expressed the theme of explanation by *symbolic modeling, precept, language symbols, words, narrative modeling, instructions, lecture presentations, undiluted narration,* and *verbal symbols* (interestingly, never the word *explanation*). He expressed the theme of demonstration by *demonstration, example, exemplification,* and *actual illustration*—fourteen different words and phrases for just two concepts.

We have revised this passage to focus it more explicitly (1) on a consistent topic string, organized around the characters *we* and *teachers,* and (2) on a few consistent thematic strings: *learn, actions, rules, demonstration,* and *explanation.*

> We learn rules for actions better when those rules are structured, whether we learn by practicing them, by watching a teacher demonstrate them, or by listening to a teacher explain them. But do we learn better from a demonstration or from an explanation? We are likely to learn more when we watch a demonstration if our language skills are so weak that we cannot understand words easily, or if the teacher cannot verbalize the rules. We are also likely to learn more from watching a demonstration when we must quickly coordinate intricate actions such as learning to ride a bicycle, but the explanation for them is too cumbersome. We may also learn more quickly from a demonstration if the action requires us to serially integrate diverse subroutines. Finally, we may learn better from a demonstration if the information is difficult or unfamiliar and the teacher lectures about it at length. In these cases, we may become satiated and not be able to pay attention. On the other hand, we will learn an action better from an explanation if we can adeptly translate explanations into actions and then store the information.

It may be that the writer of the original paragraph was remembering that familiar advice, "Vary your word choice." More bad advice. Don't strive for "elegant variation." When you use two words for one concept, you risk making your reader think you mean two concepts.

If a paragraph or passage does not seem to hang together, if it feels vague, out of focus, look at its topic and thematic strings. Its topic strings should be consistent and appropriate. Its thematic strings should be articulated clearly and concisely. There is, however, one more principle that we must observe when we introduce new topic and thematic strings.

How Do New Strings Start? Signaling Topics and Themes

Principle 3: A reader will feel that a paragraph is cohesive if he is introduced to new topic and thematic strings in a predictable location: at the end of the sentence(s) that constitute the opening section of a paragraph, section, or whole document.

Even when your paragraphs do have specific topics and thematic strings, your readers may overlook them if you do not signal them clearly. How would you characterize the following paragraph?

> Seven out of eight reigns of the Romanov line after Peter the Great were plagued by some sort of palace revolt or popular revolution. In 1722, Peter the Great passed a law of succession that terminated the principle of heredity. He proclaimed that the sovereign could appoint a successor in order to accompany his idea of achievement by merit. This resulted in many tsars not appointing a successor before dying. Even Peter the Great failed to choose someone before he died. Ivan VI was appointed by Czarina Anna, but was only two months old at his coronation in 1740. Elizabeth, daughter of Peter the Great, defeated Anna, and she ascended to the throne in 1741. Succession not dependent upon authority resulted in boyars' regularly disputing who was to become sovereign. It was not until 1797 that Paul I codified the law of succession: male primogeniture. But Paul I was strangled by conspirators, one of whom was probably his son, Alexander I.

To most readers, this paragraph seems unfocused, but its problem does not turn on missing topic or thematic strings. The paragraph consistently has characters as subject/topics, and it has three clearly stated and important thematic strings: words related to the concepts of succession, appointment, and a general theme that we might express as *turmoil*. This paragraph seems confused because in its opening sentence, its author set us up to expect one set of themes, but he delivered another. He wrote

> Seven out of eight reigns of the Romanov line after Peter the Great were plagued by some sort **of palace revolt or popular revolution.**

But he drops the theme of revolt and revolution until the last part of the paragraph, and does not explicitly articulate that theme even then. It's like hearing the overture to *Carmen* introduce *La Traviata*. He should have ended that opening sentence on the concepts that were central to his discussion: succession, appointment, turmoil.

The principle of design is this: we introduce new themes not anywhere in a sentence, but rather as close to its end as we can manage.

You'll recall that in Chapter 4 we discussed the segment at the end of a sentence—its stress position, that part of the sentence that we use to signal especially important information. We use that concluding stress position not only to emphasize important words that we think are important in that single sentence, but to signal that we intend to develop new themes in the sentences that follow. Contrast the way the evolution paragraph opens with a revision that is virtually synonymous:

> Clark's practice of carefully mapping every fossil made it possible **to follow the evolutionary development of various types through time.**

> Clark made it possible to follow the evolutionary development of various types through time because he **mapped every fossil carefully.**

The end of the original introductory sentence signals the topics and issues the writers will discuss: the topic string, which is introduced by *evolutionary development* and four thematic strings referring to the actions of the team (*follow*), to species (*various types*), to their actions (*development*), and to time (*time*). Simply by introducing those issues toward the stress position of this introductory sentence, the authors tacitly promise us that those words will be thematic keys to the rest of the paragraph. As we see them deliver on that promise, we feel we are reading a paragraph that is cohesive and coherent.

On the other hand, our revised opening sentence would set up a reader to expect a paragraph about techniques for mapping fossils carefully. This next sentence would seem to introduce a paragraph about various types of pigs:

> Because Clark mapped every fossil carefully, it was possible to follow through time the evolutionary development of **several species of pigs.**

And this next opening would set up a reader to read specifically about Clark:

> It became possible to follow through time the evolutionary development of several species of pigs because the careful mapping of every fossil had been **done by Clark.**

How we open a paragraph determines how our readers will read the rest of it, because in our opening we tell them how to frame the conceptual space that they are about to enter. To make sure they frame it in the right way, we place key thematic terms as close as we can to the end of that opening.

To revise the opening sentence of the Romanov paragraph, we would pick out the themes that in fact are important in the rest of the paragraph and then design an opening sentence that would introduce them in its stress:

> After Peter the Great died, seven out of eight reigns of the Romanov line were plagued by **turmoil over disputed succession to the throne.**

Complex Introductions

In all the preceding examples we have seen writers introduce paragraphs with a single sentence, typically called a "topic sentence." Why not just use that familiar term? One reason is that good writers often introduce paragraphs with more than just a single sentence. In the next paragraph, where does the writer seem to finish setting up her problem, to finish introducing her central issue before she begins to discuss it?

> At the outset this sum may not appear to be particularly onerous. However, the troublesome provision for violating the county ordinance against dumping toxic wastes is not the $500 fine, but the more serious mandatory penalty of "six months in county jail." Even though no jail sentences have been rendered against Abco so far, the fact that the violations are criminal in nature causes serious concern. Because the criminal aspects of these violations combine with the growing mistrust toward large, international corporations and with California's emphasis on consumerism, juries are likely to be hostile toward such actions. It is therefore appropriate that we re-evaluate the way these alleged violations are dealt with.

Most readers feel that the introduction consists of the first two sentences:

> At the outset this sum may not appear to be particularly onerous. However, the troublesome provision for violating the county ordinance against dumping toxic wastes is not the $500 fine, but the more serious mandatory penalty of "six months in county jail."

It is at the end of the second sentence that the writer introduces the topic string consisting of *jail sentences, violations, criminal aspects of these violations,* and a central thematic string consisting of *onerous, troublesome, serious, penalty, mistrust, and hostile.*

In this next paragraph the writer uses three sentences to set up her issue:

> Inflation, both of prices and of population, presented a challenge to every family in later Tudor England. One of its ironies was that in the particular economic circumstances of the time it often made a reality of what medieval people had tended to believe, that one person's good fortune was another's distress. Inflation in prices was bound to be socially divisive. The growth of population, itself the main cause of the increase in prices, ensured that those who suffered most were those most dependent on the earning of wages. But there were others, perhaps only a minority, at all social levels, whose income failed to keep pace with the rising cost of living, a situation not made easier for them to bear by the rise in the standard of material living which characterized the Elizabethan period. . . . Elizabeth's subjects, and not only those in the upper ranks of society, discovered expectations of material comfort previously undreamed of. Perhaps it was as well, in the interests of social harmony, that although new horizons were appearing, neither at home nor abroad were there really great fortunes to be made. By 1600, however, there were greater distinctions, in both town and countryside, between the rich and the poor, particularly between those of modest prosperity, the yeomen, farmers and major urban tradesmen, and the poor husbandmen, small craftsmen and full-time labourers.
>
> —Joyce Youings, *Sixteenth-Century England*[9]

It is at the end of that third sentence that Youings introduces two themes that she pursues through the paragraph: *social classes* and aspects of **divisiveness**.

> . . . Inflation in prices was bound to be *socially* divisive. The growth of population, itself the main cause of the increase in prices, ensured that **those who suffered most** were *those most dependent on the earning of wages.* But there were others, perhaps only a minority, at all *social levels,* whose **income failed to keep pace** with the rising cost of living, a situation **not made easier for them to bear** by the rise in the standard of material living which characterized the Elizabethan period. . . . Elizabeth's subjects, and not only those in *the upper ranks of society,* **discovered expectations of material comfort previously undreamed of.** Perhaps it was as well, in the interests of *social* **harmony,** that although new horizons were appearing, neither at home nor abroad were there really great fortunes to be made. By 1600, however, there **were greater distinctions,** in both town and countryside, between *the rich and the poor,* particularly *between those of modest pros-*

perity, the yeomen, farmers and major urban tradesmen, and the *poor* husbandmen, small craftsmen and full-time labourers.

In short, we can introduce new topic strings and thematic strings in a single sentence. But just as often, we create introductions consisting of two or three sentences, or (though rarely) more. To be certain that our readers do not overlook the importance of those new topic and thematic strings, we put them into the stress of the last sentence of the introduction.

These complex introductions are so common that it would be misleading to talk about "topic sentences." We have to recognize in paragraphs a more complex introductory segment. To discuss that segment, we need two new terms.

Paragraph = Issue + Discussion

Regardless of how many sentences we use to introduce the body of a paragraph (or a document or one of its sections), we have to grasp this central principle: Whether readers are conscious of it or not, they try to divide units of organized discourse—paragraphs, sections, or wholes—into two sections;

1. A short opening segment. Toward the end of this segment, in the stress position of the last sentence, readers look for the concepts the writer will discuss in the following section. Those words are often topics, but they must also include themes.

2. A longer following segment—the rest of the paragraph. In this segment, the writer develops—and readers look for—new ideas against a background of repeated topics and themes.

From time to time, we have had to find new terms to name matters that standard handbooks ignore: *nominalization, topic, stress, topic string,* etc. This complex opening segment is also ignored in most handbooks. We will call this opening segment the *issue,* and what follows it the *discussion.* The issue of a paragraph is not its ideas, its concepts, or its subject. The issue of a paragraph, of a section, or of a document is its introductory segment, its overture, if you will. The discussion typically explains, elaborates, supports, qualifies, argues for what the writer stated in the issue. The issue promises; the discussion delivers.

The issue of a paragraph may be one, two, three, or more sentences long; the issue of a section or short essay one, two, or three or more paragraphs; the issue of a long report a few pages long. But however long it is, the issue of a paragraph, section, or whole document should be short, much shorter than what it introduces. If a writer creates a disproportionately long issue, the reader may incorrectly assume that after a sentence or two, the writer has finished her introduction and is into the body of her paragraph, when in fact she is still introducing it. In longer documents, because readers risk missing where the issue stops and the discussion begins, many writers signal the end of the issue and the beginning of the discussion with a heading.

Issue is analogous to *subject* and *topic*. These three terms name introductory positions that all have the same function: to put before the reader concepts or claims that the writer intends to expand on in what follows. In the same way, the term *discussion* is analogous to *verb* and *stress*. They name the positions that follow: subject + *verb*, topic + *stress*, issue + *discussion*. And these positions all have the same function of expanding on what precedes them. In fact, we can add another level to the boxes that we have been constructing.

FIXED	ISSUE	DISCUSSION
VARIABLE	—	—

FIXED	TOPIC	STRESS
VARIABLE	OLD/FAMILIAR	NEW/UNFAMILIAR

FIXED	SUBJECT	VERB	COMPLEMENT
VARIABLE	CHARACTERS	ACTION	—

(As you can see, we have left the variable level open. We will fill it in the next chapter.)

Diagnosis and Revision

When a paragraph feels out of focus, confused, you may have one or more of four problems with its issue and discussion.

1. At the end of the issue, you introduce a concept that readers take to begin a theme, but you then fail to develop that concept in the discussion. The writer of the Romanov paragraph (p. 88) introduced in its issue the themes of *palace revolt* and *popular revolution,* but did not explicitly pursue them. He pursued instead the matters of appointment and disputed succession, and made implied references to revolt and revolution only later.

2. Conversely, you fail to anticipate in the issue important themes that you in fact develop in the discussion. The writer of the Romanov paragraph did develop some important themes in his discussion: *succession, dispute, appoint,* and a diffuse thematic string having to do with boyars' unhappiness, palace factions, and a patricidal son, a theme that we might capture in the words *trouble* or *turmoil.* But in his issue, he announced a different set of themes.

3. At the end of the issue you introduce a concept that readers think promises a theme, but in the discussion, you develop that concept using terms so varied that readers cannot connect them to your announced theme. In the demonstration/explanation paragraph (p. 86), the writer assumed that readers would understand that thirteen different terms referred to only two ideas.

4. You mention in the issue those themes that you develop in the discussion, but you bury the references to them inside a sentence, instead of highlighting them in the stress of the final sentence of the issue.

In short, if you write a passage that does not seem to hang together, seems uncentered or out of focus, you may have made a promise but didn't deliver, or you may have delivered on promises you didn't make.

Most of these problems usually result from the way most of us write our first drafts: When we draft, we are often happy just to get an opening sentence down on paper, never mind whether it sets up what follows (particularly since at that point we probably have no clear idea what in fact will follow). Only as we go on drafting the rest of the paragraph, section, or document do we begin to discover and explore some useful themes. But by that time we may be in the middle of the paragraph or essay, long past the point where our readers expected to find them.

To revise the Romanov paragraph, or any paragraph like it, we do one or all of three things:

1. Look at the discussion independently of the issue and ask what themes *in fact* the paragraph develops. Then revise the end of the issue to include any thematic strings that are present in and important to that particular discussion—in the Romanov case, the concepts referring to succession, appointment, and dispute. (A small tip: in a paragraph or essay that feels out of focus, look first at the last sentence or two. It is there that you will often find the product of your thinking and drafting. In that last sentence or two, did you use key terms that you failed to anticipate in the opening? If so, move them up to the beginning and rewrite.)

2. Deliberately weave into the discussion whatever important thematic strings you framed in the issue but omitted from the discussion. In the Romanov case it will be something more general than palace revolts and popular revolutions—*turmoil*.

3. Delete from the issue whatever you don't want to develop in the discussion. In the Romanov case, they would be specific references to palace revolts and popular revolutions. Here is Romanov revised:

> After Peter the Great died, seven out of eight reigns of the Romanov line were plagued by turmoil over disputed succession to the throne. The problems began in 1722, when Peter the Great passed a law of succession that terminated the principle of heredity and required the sovereign to appoint a successor. But because many Tsars, including Peter, died before they appointed successors, those who sought to succeed to the throne had no authority by appointment, and so their succession was regularly disputed by the boyars and other interests. There was turmoil even when successors were appointed. In 1740, Ivan VI was adopted by Czarina Anna Ivanovna and appointed as her successor at age two months, but his succession was disputed by Elizabeth, daughter of Peter the Great, who defeated Anna and her forces before ascending to the throne in 1741. In 1797 Paul tried to eliminate these disputes by codifying a new law: succession on the basis of primogeniture in the male line. But turmoil continued. Paul was strangled by conspirators, one of whom was probably Alexander I, his son.

This will win no Pulitzer Prize, but with a few changes guided by a few simple principles, we have turned a paragraph that felt disorganized and unfocused into something more coherent.

The last thing one discovers in writing a book is what to put first.
Blaise Pascal

In all pointed sentences, some degree of accuracy must be sacrificed to conciseness.
Samuel Johnson

6

Coherence II

Intentions and Points

In the last chapter, we discussed what readers look for (whether they know it or not) when they begin a paragraph, a section of a document, or a whole document: (1) They look for a relatively short opening segment that acts like an overture to what follows—we called it the *issue*. (2) Near the end of the last sentence of every issue, readers expect to find words that announce the new topics and themes that the writer will repeat in the longer segment that follows, the segment that we called the *discussion*.

In this chapter, we are going to add two more principles that will complete the third level of organization that we began with

ISSUE	DISCUSSION

To this we will add a second variable layer analogous to characters and action, to old and new information.

ISSUE	DISCUSSION
—	—

What's the Point?

> Principle 4: A reader will feel that a paragraph is coherent if she can read a sentence that specifically articulates its point.

We visibly organize essays, articles, reports, memoranda into paragraphs, subsections, and major sections to signal readers that we have finished developing one part of an idea and are moving on to another, to a new thought. But this notion of new idea or thought implies something more important than new topics and themes. When we move from one paragraph or section to another, we also imply that we intend to make some new point, to make some new claim about that new subject matter. Readers will expect to find in each paragraph and section, and also in the whole, a sentence that will be the logical, argumentative, expository center, a sentence that you could send as the telegram capturing your central idea. Here is a paragraph that was criticized for not having such a point.

> As you know, Abco is contemplating the possibility of entering into a cooperative venture with Janeway to develop an electronically controlled steering mechanism for our new line. Janeway has a long history of developing highly efficient hydraulic components including brake systems, front end systems, and various types of stabilizing systems. We have found them entirely reliable and cost-effective. So far as I know, Janeway's experience in developing electronic systems has primarily involved ignition and other engine components, not steering. The development of an electronic steering mechanism will depend on an innovative marriage of electronics and hydraulics. Edwards has recently marketed a hydraulic lift system that depends on electronic sensors to read terrain features and compensate for them. Their systems appear to have many of the features we will require in our steering mechanisms.

If we were to ask the writer of this paragraph, "So what's the point?" the writer would probably respond with something like "Well, I wanted to discuss the reasons for not committing ourselves to developing that new electronic steering system with Janeway." But when we asked about his "point," we didn't want to know what motivated him. We were asking for a sentence that we wish we had found but didn't, a sentence or two on the page that encapsulated some clear statement that we could recognize as the most important sentence in the paragraph. With this sense of "point" in mind, the writer would have responded with something like,

> Abco should not cooperate with Janeway in developing a new steering system because Edwards has more technical expertise.

And we would have said, "Well, why didn't you say that." And he would probably have replied, "It's obvious." The writer was relying on his readers to have the same set of assumptions, the same body of knowledge, the same attitudes and values that he had. Ordinarily, however, they don't.

The most common problem that writers have with points is that they fail to articulate them clearly, and so the reader doesn't get the point of a paragraph, of a section, or of the whole document. Or worse, the reader gets the wrong one.

To emphasize the difference between this general sense of what we intend and what we actually write on the page, we're going to use the word POINT in capital letters. By POINT we do not mean a general intention in the mind of the writer or the gist or summary of a passage. By POINT we mean the specific sentence on the page that the writer would send as a telegram if asked "What's your point?" In fact, the better question is not "What's your point," but "*Where's* your POINT?" In this chapter, we will discuss how careful writers make and signal POINTS for readers who do not know as much as the writer.

Where's the POINT?

> Principle 5: A reader will feel that a paragraph is coherent if he finds the POINT sentence in one of two predictable places in a paragraph: (1) at the end of its issue, or (2) at the end of its discussion; i.e., at the end of the paragraph (or section or whole document).

We'll discuss first those POINTS that appear in issues.

POINTS in Issues

Read this next paragraph, then answer the following question: if you were to pick out only one sentence *on the page* that you would send as a telegram representing the rest of the paragraph, as the POINT sentence of that paragraph, which sentence would you pick?

> Though most economists believe that business decisions are guided by a simple law of maximum profits, in fact they result from a vector of influences acting from many directions. When an advertiser selects a particular layout, for example, he depends not only on sales expectations or possible profit but also on what the present fad is. He is concerned with what colleagues and competitors will think, beliefs about the actions of the FTC, concerns

about Catholics or the American Legion, whether Chicanos or Italian-Americans will be offended, how the "silent majority" will react. He might even be worried about whether the wife or secretary of the decision maker will approve.

The answer seems straightforward—the first sentence, because it sums up the paragraph by expressing its most significant statement, the claim that the writer wants the reader to accept. The other sentences support that claim. The first sentence, then, is the POINT of this paragraph. That single POINT sentence simultaneously constitutes the entire issue of the paragraph.

Where is the POINT in this paragraph?

Our main concern was to empirically test the theory that forms the background for this work. To a great extent, we have succeeded in showing our theory is valid. Chapter Two reports a study which shows that the rate of perceiving variations in length relates directly to the number of connectives in the base structure of the text. In chapter Three, we report a study that found that subjects perceive as variable units only what the theory claims is a unit. Another series of crucial studies is the comparison and contrast experiments reported in Chapter Three, which show that we do not distinguish complex concepts of different lengths as some current theories do.

Most readers take the POINT of this paragraph to be the second sentence, again the last sentence of the issue.

What sentence captures the POINT here?

The United States is at present the world's largest exporter of agricultural products. Its agricultural net balance of payments in recent years has exceeded $10 billion a year. As rising costs of imported petroleum and other goods have increased the U.S. trade deficit, this agricultural surplus has taken on great financial importance in both the domestic and international markets. First, agricultural exports maintain profitable market prices for the American farmer and bolster the national economy by providing over one million jobs. The income from farm exports alone is used to purchase about $9 billion worth of domestic farm machinery and equipment annually. Exports of U.S. agricultural products also reduce price-depressing surpluses. Without exports, the government would be subsidizing American farmers by more than $10 billion a year over the current rate. Finally, agricultural exports provide an entry to foreign markets that can be exploited by other industries.

Most readers pick the third sentence,

> As rising costs of imported petroleum and other goods have in-
> creased the U.S. trade deficit, this agricultural surplus has taken
> on great financial importance in both the domestic and inter-
> national markets.

Once again, it is the last sentence of the issue.

When writers want to be as clear as possible, they locate their
POINTS where their readers most expect them: at the end the
issue, whether the issue is the issue of a paragraph, a section, or a
whole document.

ISSUE	DISCUSSION
POINT	

Most handbooks on writing assert that the standard paragraph begins with a "topic sentence," a sentence that announces
the subject of the paragraph (in our terms its topics and themes)
and simultaneously makes the "most general" statement (in our
terms, the POINT). But as we have just seen, a one-sentence issue
that simultaneously expresses the POINT of its paragraph is by no
means the only kind of issue. Issues may consist of one, two,
three, or in very long paragraphs, even more sentences. However
long the issue, though, readers expect POINT sentences in a predictable position: in the last sentence of an issue. This is another
reason why it is important to keep issues short. If you make your
issue very long and do not clearly signal when you finish, your
reader may take your POINT to be an earlier sentence.

What purposes are served by the sentences preceding the
POINT? They typically provide transition from a previous paragraph, make a general claim that the writer will narrow in the
POINT, or make a preliminary claim that the POINT sentence rejects. In the following two-sentence issue, sentence (1) is a transition, sentence (2) is the POINT:

> (1) We can put this abstract notion of issue in simpler terms. (2)
> Think of an issue as the overture to an opera, in which the com-
> poser announces the themes that he will repeat, modulate, com-
> bine, and develop in a variety of interesting ways.

In this next three-sentence issue, sentences (1–2) constitute a generalization that is narrowed in POINT sentence (3):

> (1) Writing well involves so many skills that it is hard to know where to begin describing what makes a good writer. (2) Among other considerations, a writer must be sensitive to words, style, organization, subject matter, logic, emotion, audience. (3) Perhaps the most crucial of these, though, is a sensibility to one's audience, to how readers read.

In this next two-sentence issue, sentence (1) is a claim that POINT-sentence (2) rejects:

> (1) Most high school teachers think that good paragraphs must have a single topic sentence that introduces the paragraph. (2) But that is evidently not so because professional writers regularly introduce their paragraphs with two or more sentences.

Writers do not always, however, locate their POINT sentences in the issue of their paragraphs, sections, and documents. Sometimes, they put POINT sentences at the end of their discussion.

POINTS at the Ends of Discussions

Most paragraphs are POINT-early, their POINTS typically appearing as the last sentence of their issue. But that is only a statistical observation. We can also put a POINT at the end of a paragraph, at the end of the discussion, and still seem entirely coherent. Here is a paragraph whose POINT is at the end:

> Something has happened to the American male's need to display the signs of stereotypical masculinity that once seemed necessary for survival on the frontier. For a long time, American males were confident in their manhood, sure of their sexual roles and images. Indeed, the rugged frontiersmen never even thought about their masculinity; they were simply men surviving in a dangerous world and dressing the part. Then in the nineteenth century, our ideal male became the cowboy, then the world adventurer, then the war hero. They all were confident of themselves and unselfconsciously dressed their part. But in this century, something happened: Hemingway's heroes, for example, seemed to feel that they had to prove that it was still important to be a man among men, and our image of them is one of a kind of Brooks Brothers ruggedness. They seemed less confident that their masculinity had a real function. Now one can detect a new theme: as the male image as conqueror and survivor has lost its value, men have felt free to

dress in ways once thought feminine, to wear earrings, even to wear makeup. These signs of a change in the American male's sexual image of himself suggests something deeper than changes in appearance: he is adapting to a world in which the image of traditional masculinity is no longer necessary for survival.

But if the writer does put the POINT sentence at the end of the discussion of the paragraph (or section or document), in its issue he must still use its issue to introduce the discussion in a way that anticipates its topics and themes. In this paragraph, the issue is its first sentence. But while the writer does not assert the POINT of the paragraph in its issue, he does introduce its key topics and themes:

> Something has happened to the American male's need to **display** the **signs** of **stereotypical masculinity** that once seemed necessary for **survival** on the frontier.

Why put a POINT sentence last in a paragraph? Usually, the writer wants to develop her argument before making her claim. Sometimes she discovers it there (more about this in a moment). But predictably, a writer will put her POINT sentence at the end of the paragraph because she intends to develop, expand, elaborate, explore that POINT in the following series of paragraphs. In fact, if the writer uses the paragraph to introduce a whole document, then she will predictably locate her POINT at the end of that paragraph.

Introductory Paragraphs: A Special Problem

Here is a typical opening paragraph:

> Man's fascination with machines that move under their own power and control is at least as old as recorded history. In Aristotle's Greece, plays of several acts are said to have been performed entirely by automatic puppets driven by weights hung on twisted cords. Much later European royalties were enthralled by lifelike automata that could write, draw, and play musical instruments. In recent years most of the magical aura surrounding mechanical automata has been dispelled. Today automatic machines and industrial robots are used in factories throughout the world to perform tasks that are too hazardous, too onerous, too boring or simply too uneconomic for human beings to undertake.

The issue of this paragraph appears to be the first sentence. It introduces the topics and themes of history, fascination, and machines that move under their own power. In the discussion, the writer develops and expands those themes and topics, offering historical examples of automatic machines, gradually narrowing down to modern robots. But it is the last sentence to which the writer wants us to give the most rhetorical weight. The rest of the article is specifically about modern uses of robots in contexts that to humans are dangerous, onerous, boring, or uneconomical.

In a single opening paragraph such as this, a paragraph that constitutes the issue to everything that follows, the writer typically locates the main POINT sentence at the end of the paragraph, in the last sentence. And if the opening of an article or report consists of more than one paragraph, then the main POINT sentences will appear at the end of the whole opening.

POINTS in Whole Documents

We have made two generalizations about where to put POINT sentences in paragraphs:

1. If the paragraph is a body paragraph, if it does not introduce a section or whole document, you can make your POINT sentence in either or both of two places: (a) at the end of the introductory issue, and (b) at the end of the paragraph; i.e., at the end of the discussion.

2. But if the paragraph introduces a section or even a whole document, then you should put your POINT sentence at the end of that paragraph.

How do these principles apply to documents? The translation is simple: in documents, you can make your POINT either

1. At the end of the issue (then again at the end of the document).

2. At the end of the document.

But as readers, we may have a problem with a document whose main POINT is at the end: when we begin reading the document, we cannot always be certain whether the sentence(s) that we find at the end of the issue are the main POINT sentences of the whole document, or whether we will find a more important main POINT sentence at the end of the document. Look at this paragraph about scaffolding and Abco's liability:

You have asked me to determine the matter of Abco's potential liability for the plaintiff's injuries claimed as a result of his climbing Abco's scaffolding. To determine Abco's potential liability we must analyze four factors. They are (1) did Abco construct the scaffolding negligently; (2) did Abco provide adequate assembly instructions; (3) did plaintiff assemble the scaffolding according to the instructions; and (4) did the plaintiff use the scaffolding in a manner prescribed in the instructions?

If this is the issue to the whole memo, then the last sentence listing the questions to be answered *could* be the main POINT sentence of the whole document. If so, the person who assigned the task would judge the writer to be incompetent, because he didn't answer the *real* question—Is Abco liable? On the other hand, the writer might go on to make the main POINT at the end of the memo; if so, he would thereby have created a POINT-last document.

If that were the case, then the sentence about the four kinds of analyses at the end of the issue becomes an *anticipatory* POINT, a minor POINT intended only to launch the reader into the rest of the document, to anticipate and frame the discussion by announcing themes and topics. Always observe this principle: if you make your POINT at the end of a document, you must still offer the reader an anticipatory POINT.

In general, however, most readers in most nonacademic situations don't like that kind of organization. They want to see the POINT up front. So unless you can justify creating a POINT-last document (see below for some reasons), don't do it. But if you must, then you should observe two more principles of construction. At the end of the introductory issue of your document, you must,

1. offer some kind of specific anticipatory POINT sentence(s) that clearly promise a main POINT still to come; and

2. include toward the end of that anticipatory POINT sentence the themes and topics that you will pursue.

Whether you make your POINT early or late, you must always frame the space that your reader is about to enter.

Why POINT-last Documents?

Writers usually offer one of three reasons for deliberately locating their main POINT sentences at the end of a document. There is a fourth, one to which they usually do not admit.

Timidity or Politeness. Some professionals believe that if a document delivers bad news, they should withhold the main POINT until the end. The theory is that if the writer can gently walk her readers through her reasoning toward the unwelcome POINT, the reader will be more willing to accept it. When a writer feels that she has to deliver a POINT that is unpopular, controversial, or nasty, or when she feels that she does not have the authority simply to deliver her POINT outright and make it stick, she may feel that before she delivers the bad news she has to lay down a foundation of history, evidence, and reasoning. That's not a matter of style; it's a matter of judgment, nerve, character, or standing. In fact, most professionals prefer POINT-first documents, no matter how bad the news.

Discovery. Sometimes writers put their main POINT sentences last because they want their readers to work through an argument or a body of data to experience a sense of discovery. They believe that the development of the POINT is as important as the POINT itself. In fact, that kind of organization characterizes parts of this book: we have frequently begun with some contrasting passages to develop a small-p point, in the hope that you would grasp it a moment before you read the POINT sentence.

As we have emphasized, though, most readers in most professional contexts prefer documents with main POINT early. Articles in many sciences—hard or soft—begin with abstracts that typically contain the POINT of the article. Readers in those areas also know that, after reading the abstract, they can go directly to the conclusion if they want to see the main POINT expressed in more detail. These readers employ a reading strategy that creates a POINT-first form: if they don't find the POINT on the first page, they flip to the conclusion, where they expect to find it.

Convention. Writers put a main POINT last when local convention encourages it, typically in the belletristic essay. In some fields outside the sciences, it is typical for a writer first to announce (some would say invent) a problem that no one suspected until the writer pointed it out. In this kind of writing, obviously enough, the writer is under no pressure to answer a question that no one except the writer has asked. But once the writer has convinced us of an unsuspected problem with, say, gender roles in the third book of Milton's *Paradise Lost*, she then sets to working through the problem, demonstrating how inventively she is solving it, how much more complex the problem is than we might have thought even from her early account of it. Only after we have accompanied the writer through her argument do we begin to catch sight of her main POINT.

In fact, most readers of belletristic prose would find the alternative POINT-early organization too crude, too flatfooted. And we cooperate with writers in this convention by the way we read: before we decide whether to read a piece by, say, Norman Mailer in *The New York Review of Books,* we do not flip to its end to see whether we find his conclusion interesting and only then decide to read the whole piece. But those who read scientific journals do that regularly when they read articles in those journals. Habits of reading are as conventionalized as habits of writing.

But again, this kind of main POINT-last writing is distinctly disfavored in most other kinds of professional discourse in our culture. We say "in our culture" because in some cultures, it is considered discourteous to state a POINT clearly and directly at all, much less early. It is one of the problems that Americans have reading discourse written in those cultures, and that writers from those cultures often have when they try to write documents for American readers. We are trained to look for POINTS; others are trained to avoid them.

There is a fourth reason why writers make their main POINTS at the end of a discourse rather than at the beginning.

Failure to Revise. We've suggested this problem earlier. When we draft, we often have no idea where we are going, what kind of POINT sentence we are going to write, until we discover it at the end of a paragraph, section, or even the whole document. If we do not revise that kind of document, we offer our reader only a running account of our thinking. If you look over a document and discover that your main POINT is last, not by design, but as an accident of your having discovered it there, and you are writing for an audience not interested in a narrative account of your mental life, revise. Move the main POINT to the end of your introductory issue. Then start the kind of revision that we did with the Romanov paragraph: track down topics and themes, delete misleading words and terms, weave into your issue and discussion key topics and themes.

Our best advice is this: Unless you have good reason to withhold your main POINTS until the end, get them out early—but not immediately, not before you get to the end of a reasonably concise introductory issue. Make sure that a main POINT sentence encapsulates what you take to be your major claim, observation, proposition, idea, request, warning, direction, command—a sentence that you would send to your reader if you had only a post card to write it on. In those encapsulating sentence(s), be sure that you express toward the end whatever thematic or topic strings you want your readers to notice thereafter.

The Model Entire

With this discussion of POINT, we can now complete our set of boxes. In our first four chapters, we developed a simple way to represent the apparently natural connections between subjects and characters, between verbs and actions, among topics and old information and characters, and between stress and new information. We then added a half of a third level, the layer of issue and discussion and put the POINT specifically at the end of the issue, because there must always be one there.

But because we must also locate our main POINTS at the end of an introductory paragraph, we have to add one more variable:

ISSUE	DISCUSSION
POINT	(POINT)

As we write, we are always trying to find the best place to locate those elements that we can move: characters, actions, old and new information. We put these variable elements in parts of sentences that have a fixed order: subject + verb, topic + stress. In the same way, as we write, we always have to decide where we are going to make our POINT: at the end of the issue, or at the end of the discussion. Readers find writing to be clear, direct, and readable to the degree that they find central characters in subjects, old information in topics, and POINTS at the ends of issues; when they find crucial actions in verbs, new and important information in the stress, and *certain* POINTS at the ends of discussions.

We can compress a substantial amount of information about clarity and organization into a single complex figure:

ISSUE	DISCUSSION
POINT	(POINT)

TOPIC	STRESS
OLD/FAMILIAR	NEW/UNFAMILIAR

SUBJECT	VERB	COMPLEMENT
CHARACTERS	ACTION	—

To this figure we add three principles:

1. In the issue, introduce key thematic and topical words in its stress.

2. In the discussion, keep strings of topics consistent.

3. In the discussion, repeat those thematic words or words related to them.

We can use these principles both to predict when our readers might judge our writing to be cloudy and to achieve what we might call generic clarity. We achieve an individual style when we learn how to meet the expectations of our readers, and at the same time surprise them.

The final point is not to make every paragraph a work of art. Art may be long, but life is too short. The point is to make these principles work together *well enough* so that you do not confuse your readers. Readers call writing clear not when it *is* clear, but when they have no reason to call it unclear. Which is to say, writing usually seems clearest when readers are least conscious of it.

Headings as Test for Coherence

Headings are a familiar feature in professional writing. We usually think of them as most helpful to readers, because they give readers a general idea about the content of the section they head. They also show readers where one section stops and another starts and indicate levels of subordination.

But if headings are useful to readers, they are more useful to writers, because writers can use them to diagnose potential problems with the perceived structure of a document.

The Location of Headings

1. Locate in your document where you would insert a heading to signal the end of your issue and the beginning of your discussion. At this point, don't worry about what should go into the heading; just locate where it should be.

2. In the body of the discussion, locate places where you would insert at least one more equivalent level of headings.

3. Repeat for each section until you have a heading at least every three or four pages.

How many places you find will depend on how long your document is. A ten-page document might have only two or three headings in the discussion. A longer one will have more.

Now, if you could not quickly and confidently find those places where you would insert headings, you have a problem: you don't know where the major junctures are in your own document. If you can't identify them, neither will your readers.

The Content of Headings

Once you have located where headings should go, you can decide on their specific words. The words in a heading should state the new and central topics and themes of each section. To determine what those topics and themes should be, simply look at the ends of your issues, at the stress of your POINTS. If you do that and you still don't know what should be the words in your headings, you have a problem, because if you cannot identify your own key concepts, neither will your readers.

Finally, consider the highest heading of all: your title. What should go into a useful title is straightforward: the key topics and themes that appear in the stress of your main POINT sentence. Two-part titles are fashionable,

Computer Assisted Instruction: Advantages and Disadvantages

but they are also useful. If you don't get the key themes and topics in the first part, you might get them in the second.

Not all readers like headings; some feel they give a crude vocational look to writing, that good readers don't need them.

Whatever your feelings, you ought not to underestimate how useful they are as a way to anticipate how your readers are likely to respond to the form of your paper. If you are not certain where to locate headings, if you are not certain what words to put into those headings, you can be certain that your readers will find your document confusing. If you think headings are déclassé, you can always delete them.

A Final Note on Drafting

Almost everything that we have discussed so far has to do with examining what you have drafted—interrogating it, looking at your answers, and then if the answers so indicate, with revising it. These last two chapters on coherence, though, also suggest ways you can think about your problem even before you begin to draft.

Before you begin, you know that you will eventually have to write a POINT sentence that your readers will recognize and judge important; you know that your POINT sentence will have key words that express central concepts that your readers must recognize as central if they are to make sense out of what follows. Before you begin to draft, then, there are a few things you might do so that you can draft productively.

1. List your main characters, including any abstractions that seem to act as sources of action. Decide which characters will most interest your audience, decide whose point of view you want to take. The point of view defined by those characters will constitute most of the topics in your topic strings.

2. List a few central concepts that you think will run through your whole text. Then around each of those key concepts create clusters of additional concepts. The words for those central and subordinate concepts will provide many of your thematic strings.

3. If you think you know exactly what has to go into your POINT sentence, write it out. Specifically use the characters that will constitute your major topic strings and the key concepts that will be the center of your clusters. Recall that the central conceptual terms will go toward the end of that POINT sentence. (If you don't know your POINT go to (8).)

4. Subdivide the problem into manageable segments with their particular thematic strings and characters.

5. Before you write the first word, decide whether the document is going to be POINT-early or POINT-last.

6. If POINT-last, construct an anticipatory POINT sentence to get started. It too should have key thematic terms in it.

7. As you draft, occasionally remind yourself of your thematic and topic strings.

8. If you don't know your POINT, just start writing and hope.

9. Once you have produced a first draft, determine whether the POINT sentence in the draft is the same as the POINT sentence you wrote before you began to draft. Look particularly for new words in the POINT in your conclusion.

10. If they are different, which does the job better? It is likely that in the act of drafting you will have discovered something more interesting, more compelling, more pointed than you thought before you began.

11. At this stage in the process, you can begin the more detailed diagnostic work that goes into effective revision.

Less is more.
Robert Browning

There is no artifice as good and desirable as simplicity.
St. Francis De Sales

Loquacity and lying are cousins.
German Proverb

To a Snail: If "compression is the first grace of style," you have it.
Marianne Moore

If you require a practical rule of me, I will present you with this: Whenever you feel an impulse to perpetrate a piece of exceptionally fine writing, obey it—wholeheartedly—and delete it before sending your manuscript to press. Murder your darlings.
Arthur Quiller-Couch

In composing, as a general rule, run your pen through every other word you have written; you have no idea what vigour it will give your style.
Sydney Smith

Everything should be made as simple as possible, but not simpler.
Albert Einstein

7

Concision

Once you can use the structure of a sentence and a paragraph to organize your ideas, you're a long way toward a clear and direct style. But some sentences and paragraphs enjoy all the virtues of grammatical clarity yet remain wordy and graceless. Even when you arrange their parts in all the right ways, they can still succumb to acute prolixity:

> The point I want to make here is that we can see that American policy in regard to foreign countries as the State Department in Washington and the White House have put it together and made it public to the world has given material and moral support to too many foreign factions in other countries that have controlled power and have then had to give up the power to other factions that have defeated them.

That is,

> Our foreign policy has backed too many losers.

In the longer version, the writer matches agents and actions to subjects and verbs. But she uses ten words where one would have served.

To write clearly, we have to know not only how to manage the flow of ideas but also how to express them concisely. These two principles are easier to state than to follow.

1. Usually, compress what you mean into the fewest words.
2. Don't state what your reader can easily infer.

We inflate our prose in so many ways that it's no use trying to list them all. But you might find it helpful to know the most common kinds of wordiness. This sentence illustrates most of them:

> In my personal opinion, we must listen to and think over in a punctilious manner each and every suggestion that is offered to us.

First, an opinion can only be personal, so we can cut *personal*. And since any statement is implicitly opinion, we can cut *in my opinion. Listen to and think over* means *consider,* and *in a punctilious manner* means *punctiliously,* which means no more than *carefully. Each and every* is a redundant pair; we need only *each.* A *suggestion* is by definition something offered, and offered to someone, so neither do we need *that is offered to us.* What's left is much leaner,

> We must consider each suggestion carefully.

Simple Sources of Wordiness

In the following cases, you can just cross out useless words. You will have to rewrite little, if at all.

Redundant Pairs

English has a long tradition of doubling words, a habit that we acquired shortly after we began to borrow from Latin and French the thousands of words that we have since incorporated into English. Because the borrowed word usually sounded a bit more learned than the familiar native one, early writers would use both. Among the common pairs are *full and complete, true and accurate, hopes and desires, hope and trust, each and every, first and foremost, any and all, various and sundry, basic and fundamental, questions and problems,* and, *and so on and so forth.* Some standard pairs are not redundant: *willing and able.*

Redundant Modifiers

Every word implies another. *Finish* implies *complete,* so *completely finish* is redundant. *Memories* imply *past,* so *past memories* is redundant. *Different* implies *various,* so *various different* is redundant. *Each* implies *individual,* so *each individual* is redundant. Other examples are *basic fundamentals, true facts, important essentials, future plans, personal beliefs, consensus of opinion, sudden crisis, terrible tragedy, end result, final outcome, initial preparation, free gift.* In every case, we simply prune the redundant modifier. Compare:

> We should not try to anticipate **in advance** those great events that will **completely** revolutionize our society because **past** history tells us that it has been the **ultimate** outcome of little events that has **unexpectedly** surprised us.

> We should not try to anticipate great events that will revolutionize our society because history tells us that the effect of little events has most surprised us.

In many cases, the preposition alone is redundant: revolve *around*, return *back*, penetrate *into*, split *apart*, progress *forward*, continue *on*. But some verb + preposition combinations are now so idiomatic that we would sound odd if we did not add them: *stand up, sit down, lie down, watch over*.

Redundant Categories

Specific words imply their general categories, so we usually don't have to state both. We know that time is a period, that the mucous membrane is an area, that pink is a color, and that shiny is an appearance. So we don't have to write,

> During that **period of time**, the **mucous membrane area** became **pink in color** and **shiny in appearance**.

but only,

> During that **time**, the **mucous membrane** became **pink and shiny**.

In some cases, we can eliminate a general category by changing an adjective into an adverb:

> The holes must be aligned in an **accurate manner**.

> The holes must be **accurately** aligned.

And in some cases, we can change an adjective into a noun and drop the redundant noun:

> The **educational process** and **athletic activities** are the responsibility of **county governmental systems**.

> **Education** and **athletics** are the responsibility of **county governments**.

In each case we delete the general noun and leave the more specific word.

Here are some general nouns often used redundantly. In every case, we can be more direct and concise by dropping the general word:

> large in **size**, of a bright **color**, heavy in **weight**, round in **shape**, at an early **time**

of a cheap **quality,** honest in **character,** of an uncertain **condition,** in a confused **state,** unusual in **nature,** extreme in **degree,** of a strange **type**

curative **process,** regulation **system,** economics **field, area** of mathematics, criminal **problem.**

Meaningless Modifiers

Some modifiers are verbal tics that we use almost as unconsciously as we clear our throats—words and phrases such as kind of, really, basically, definitely, practically, actually, virtually, generally, certain, particular, individual, given, various, different, specific, for all intents and purposes.

> **For all intents and purposes,** American industrial productivity **generally** depends on **certain** factors that are **really** more psychological **in kind** than of any **given** technological aspect.

When we prune both the empty nouns and meaningless modifiers, we have a clearer and sharper sentence:

> American industrial productivity depends more on psychology than on technology.

Pompous Diction

Replacing unnecessarily formal words with more common ones may not reduce wordiness, but you will make your diction sharper and more direct.

> Pursuant to the recent memorandum issued August 9, 1989, because of financial exigencies, it is incumbent upon us all to endeavor to make maximal utilization of telephonic communication in lieu of personal visitation.

All of that means only,

> As the memo of August 9 said, to save the company money, use the telephone as much as you can instead of making personal visits.

There is a common word for almost every fancy borrowed one. When we pick the ordinary word we rarely lose anything important.

Sometimes, of course, the more obscure, more formal word is exactly the right one:

> We tried to negotiate in good faith but the union remains utterly
> intransigent.

Intransigent is not synonymous with *stubborn* or *firm* or *fixed*
or *unyielding* or *uncompromising*. It means to adopt an *unrea-
sonably* fixed position. We can, for example, be uncompromising
about our moral behavior, but we would not want to say that we
were intransigent about it, for that would suggest that we *should*
compromise. So if we mean intransigent, then we should use
intransigent.

A smattering of big words and their simpler near-synonyms:

Contingent upon—dependent on

Endeavor—try

Utilization—use

Termination—end

Initiate—begin

Is desirous of—wants

Cognizant of—aware of

Ascertain—find out

Facilitate—help

Implement—start, carry out, begin

Deem—think

Envisage—think, regard, see

Advert to—mention

Apprise—inform

Eventuate—happen

Transpire—happen

Render—make, give

Transmit—send

Prior to—before

Subsequent to—after

Complex Wordiness

In these next cases, you have to think about your prose more
carefully and then rewrite more extensively.

Belaboring the Obvious. Often, we are diffusely redundant,
needlessly stating what everyone knows:

> Imagine a picture of someone engaged in the activity of trying to
> learn the rules for playing the game of chess.

Imagine implies *picture; trying to learn* implies *engaged in an
activity; chess* implies *game; game* implies *playing.* The less redundant version:

> Imagine someone trying to learn the rules of chess.

Or consider this:

> When you write down your ideas, keep in mind that the audience
> that reads what you have to say will infer from your writing style
> something about your character.

You can write down only ideas; your audience can read only what you have to say; you write only to them; they can infer something about your character only from your writing. So in fewer words,

> Keep in mind that your readers will infer from your style something about your character.

Excessive Detail. Other kinds of redundancy are more difficult to prune. Sometimes, we provide irrelevant details.

> Baseball, one of our oldest and most popular outdoor summer sports in terms of total attendance at ball parks and viewing on television, has the kind of rhythm of play on the field that alternates between the players' passively waiting with no action taking place between the pitches to the batter and exploding into action when the batter hits a pitched ball to one of the players and he fields it.

That is,

> Baseball has a rhythm that alternates between waiting and explosive action.

How much detail we should provide depends on how much our readers already know. In technical writing addressed to an informed audience, we can usually assume a good deal of shared knowledge.

> The basic type results from simple rearrangement of the phonemic content of polysyllabic forms so that the initial CV of the first stem syllable is transposed with the first CV of the second stem syllable.

The writer didn't bother to define *phonemic content, stem syllable,* or *CV* because he assumed that anyone reading a technical linguistics journal would understand those terms.

On the other hand, this definition of *phonetic transcription,* which would never appear in a technical journal on language, is necessary in an introductory textbook:

> To study language scientifically, we need some kind of phonetic transcription, a system to write a language so that visual symbols consistently represent segments of speech.

Concise writing involves more than pruning redundancy or avoiding excessive detail, because in some situations, the writer may have no idea what counts as redundant or excessive. Every teacher of freshman English has seen papers that begin with a sentence on the order of "Shakespeare, who wrote *Macbeth,* wrote many other famous plays." Tell the student that he doesn't have to say that and he is likely to answer, "Why not? It's true, isn't it?" You say, "Well, yes, but you just don't have to say it. It's obvious." Moment of thoughtful silence. "What else shouldn't I say?"

We signal that we are members of a community in what we say and how we say it. But a more certain sign of our socialization is in what we don't say, in what we take for granted as part of a shared but rarely articulated body of knowledge and values. Here, for example, is the first paragraph from the first paper written by someone who was by no means a novice to writing but who was a novice in the community he had just joined. He was a first-year law student at a very selective school of law, a student who had the June before graduated very nearly at the top of his class from a prestigious college, and who in that community had been perceived as an entirely competent writer (I know because I looked up his record):

> It is my opinion that the ruling of the lower court concerning the case of *Haslem* v. *Lockwood* should be upheld, thereby denying the appeal of the plaintiff. The main point supporting my point of view on this case concerns the tenet of our court system which holds that in order to win his case, the plaintiff must prove that he was somehow wronged by the defendant. The burden of proof rests on the plaintiff. He must show enough evidence to convince the court that he is in the right.

To his first-year legal writing instructor, this paragraph was a tissue of self-evident truisms, all redundant, all "filler." Obviously if the original ruling is upheld, the appeal is denied; obviously the plaintiff can win his case only if he can prove he was wronged by the defendant; obviously the burden of proof rests with the plaintiff; obviously the plaintiff has to provide the court with evidence. But at this point in his academic career, the writer had not yet so thoroughly assimilated that knowledge that he could unselfconsciously resist stating it.

Viewed from a wider perspective, this kind of belaboring the obvious has a function. When writers articulate the obvious in speech or in writing, they help themselves learn that information. One way we get knowledge under control is by writing it out.

Those of us who are already socialized in a field should think twice before we dismiss as incompetent a writer who seems wordy or banal. He may be, but he may also simply be learning his stuff.

The larger-scale version of this problem is a paper or memo or study that seems to be all "summary" when we explicitly asked— or were asked for—"analysis." It may be that the writer who only summarizes in fact does not know the difference between summary and analysis or is so intellectually incompetent that he cannot analyze at all. But it may also be that before most writers can analyze anything new and complex, they have to articulate it, to summarize it in writing. Anyone with an expert's knowledge in a field can scan a text, quickly grasp and incorporate its new content into her familiar knowledge, and then easily criticize (i.e., analyze) the text. A novice no less intelligent, with a memory just as powerful, will be able to recall much less from merely scanning that text, and will certainly not be able to manipulate its information and argument in any analytical way.

There is a theory of learning that we might call the "velcro theory of knowledge." The more old knowledge we have about a subject, the more new knowledge we can retain (1) because new knowledge sticks to old knowledge, and (2) because if we are rich in knowledge about a subject, we probably have organized that knowledge in a way that allows us to incorporate new knowledge into it quickly and efficiently. But if we are novices, if we do not have that rich and well structured base of knowledge, we are more likely to feel that we have to instantiate and rehearse that knowledge on a page before we can get it under control in our minds. (And even if we are knowledgeable in a field, we may find it easier to get new knowledge under control by writing it out, even if we never use that summary in a final draft.)

A Phrase for a Word.   The redundancy we've described so far results when we state what we could have left implied, a problem we can edit away simply by testing the need for every word and phrase. But another kind of redundancy is more difficult to revise, because to do so we need a precise vocabulary and the wit to use it. For example,

> As you carefully read what you have written to improve your wording and catch small errors of spelling, punctuation, and so on, the thing to do before you do anything else is to try to see

where sequences of subjects and verbs could replace the same ideas expressed in nouns rather than verbs.

In other words,

As you edit, first find nominalizations you can replace with clauses.

We have compressed several words into single words:

carefully read what you have written . . . and so on	= edit
the thing to do before you do anything else	= first
try to see where . . . are	= find
sequences of subjects and verbs	= clauses
the same ideas expressed in nouns rather than verbs	= nominalizations

There are no general rules to tell you when you can compress several words into a word or two. I can only point out that you often can, and that you should be on the alert for opportunities to do so—which is to say, try.

You can compress many common phrases:

the reason for for the reason that due to the fact that owing to the fact that in light of the fact that considering the fact that on the grounds that this is why	because, since, why

It is difficult to explain **the reason for** the delay in the completion of the investigation.
It is difficult to explain **why**. . . .

In light of the fact that no profits were reported from 1967 through 1974, the stock values remained largely unchanged.
Because no profits were reported. . . .

despite the fact that regardless of the fact that notwithstanding the fact that	although, even though

Despite the fact that the results were checked several times, serious errors crept into the findings.
Even though the results. . . .

in the event that if it should transpire/happen that under circumstances in which	if

In the event that the materials arrive after the scheduled date, contact the shipping department immediately.
If the materials arrive. . . .

on the occasion of
in a situation in which   } when
under circumstances in which

In a situation in which a class is overenrolled, you may request that the instructor reopen the class.
When a class is overenrolled. . . .

as regards
in reference to
with regard to   } about
concerning the matter of
where _____ is concerned

I should now like to make a few observations **concerning the matter of** contingency funds.
I should now like to make a few observations **about** contingency funds.

it is crucial that
it is necessary that
there is a need/necessity for   } must, should
it is important that
it is incumbent upon
cannot be avoided

There is a need for more careful inspection of all welds.
You **must** inspect all welds more carefully.
Inspect all welds more carefully.

It is important that the proposed North-South Thruway not displace significant numbers of residents.
The proposed North-South Thruway **must** not displace significant numbers of residents.

is able to
is in a position to
has the opportunity to   } can
has the capacity for
has the ability to

We are in a position to make you a firm offer for your house.
We can make you a firm offer for your house.

it is possible that
there is a chance that
it could happen that   } may, might, can, could
the possibility exists for

It is possible that nothing will come of these preparations.
Nothing **may** come of these preparations.

| prior to
in anticipation of
subsequent to
following on
at the same time as
simultaneously with | before, after, as |

Prior to the expiration of the apprenticeship period, it is incumbent upon you to make application for full membership.
Before your apprenticeship expires, apply for full membership.

| increase
decrease | more, less/fewer; better, worse |

There has been an **increase** in the number of universities offering adult education programs.
More universities are offering adult education programs.

We have noted a **decrease** in the quality of applicants.
We have noted that applicants are **less** qualified.

Metadiscourse, One More Time

In Chapter 2, we described metadiscourse as the language we use when we refer to our own thinking and writing as we think and write—*to summarize, on the contrary, I believe;* to the structure of what we write—*first, second, more importantly;* and to our reader's act of reading—*note that, consider now, in order to understand.* We use metadiscourse in personal narratives, arguments, memoirs—in any discourse in which we filter our ideas through a concern with how our reader will take them. Except for numbers that indicate sections and so on, there is less metadiscourse in other kinds of writing—operating instructions, technical manuals, laws, and the like.

The problem is to recognize when metadiscourse is useful and then to control it. Some writers use so much metadiscourse that they bury their ideas. For example:

> The last point I would like to make here is that in regard to men-women relationships, it is important to keep in mind that the greatest changes have probably occurred in the way men and women seem to be working next to one another.

Only part of that sentence addresses men-women relationships:

> . . . greatest changes have . . . occurred in the way men and women . . . working next to one another.

The rest tells readers how to understand what they are reading:

> The last point I would like to make here is that in regard to . . . it
> is important to keep in mind that . . . probably . . . seem to . . .

Pruned of the writing about reading, the sentence becomes more
direct:

> The greatest changes in men-women relationships have occurred
> in the way men and women work next to one another.

And now that we can see what this sentence really says, we can
make it more direct:

> Men and women have changed their relationships most in the
> way they work together.

In deciding how much metadiscourse to include, we can't rely
on broad generalizations. Some entirely successful writers use a
good deal; others equally successful, very little. Read widely in
your field with an eye to how metadiscourse is used by writers
you think are clear, concise, and successful. Then do likewise.

Here are some of the more common types of metadiscourse.

Hedges and Emphatics

Each profession has its own idiom of caution and confidence.
None of us wants to sound like an uncertain milquetoast or a
smug dogmatist. How successfully we walk the rhetorical line
between seeming timidity and arrogance depends a good deal on
how we manage phrases like *a good deal,* a phrase that a few
words ago allowed me to pull back from the more absolute
statement:

> How successfully we walk the rhetorical line between seeming
> timidity and arrogance depends on how we manage phrases like **a
> good deal.**

Hedges let us sound small notes of civilized diffidence. They
give us room to backpedal and to make exceptions. An appropriate emphatic, on the other hand, lets us underscore what we
really believe—or would like our reader to think we believe.

Some of the more common hedges: *usually, often, sometimes,
almost, virtually, possibly, perhaps, apparently, seemingly, in*

some ways, to a certain extent, sort of, somewhat, more or less, for the most part, for all intents and purposes, in some respects, in my opinion at least, may, might, can, could, seem, tend, try, attempt, seek, hope. Some of us use these so often that they become less hedges than meaningless modifiers.

Some of the more common emphatics: *as everyone knows, it is generally agreed that, it is quite true that, it's clear that, it is obvious that, the fact is, as we can plainly see, literally, clearly, obviously, undoubtedly, certainly, of course, indeed, inevitably, very, invariably, always, key, central, crucial, basic, fundamental, major, cardinal, primary, principal, essential.* Words and phrases like these generally mean not much more than "believe me." Used to excess, they make us seem arrogant or at least defensive. Or they become a kind of background static that robs a style of any clarity or precision. This is another case where a good ear will serve you better than a flat rule.

Sequencers and Topicalizers

Sequencers and topicalizers are words, phrases, and sentences that lead your reader through your text. The least useful kind are overelaborate introductions:

> In this next section of this report, it is my intention to deal with the problem of noise pollution. The first thing I want to say is that noise pollution is. . . .

You can announce the topic of a whole discourse—or any of its parts—and hint at the structure of its argument more simply:

> The next problem is noise pollution. It . . .

Unless your paper is so complex that you have to lay out its plan in an elaborate introduction, assume that just naming the problem is sufficient to announce it as your topic, and that naming its parts suggests your organization.

Look carefully at introductory sentences that you begin with a metadiscourse subject and verb that are followed by a topic to be discussed:

> In this essay, I will discuss **Robert Frost's clumsy use of Freudian images in his early poems.**

Almost always, this kind of sentence can be revised into a straight-forward point that doesn't need an introduction announcing the writer's intentions:

> In his early poems, Robert Frost used Freudian images clumsily.

In fact, this kind of revision can reveal the absence of a point.

> In this report, I will analyze GM's tactics in its acquisition of domestic suppliers.

This revises into something fairly pointless.

> GM uses tactics when it acquires domestic suppliers.

Attributors and Narrators

Attributors and narrators tell your reader where you got your ideas or facts or opinions. Sometimes, when we are still trying to work out precisely what it is we want to say, we offer a narrative of our thinking rather than its results:

> **I was concerned with** the structural integrity of the roof supports, so **I attempted** to test the weight that the transverse beams would carry. **I have concluded** after numerous tests that the beams are sufficiently strong to carry the prescribed weight, but no more. **I think** that it is important that we notify every section that uses the facility of this finding.

If we eliminate the narrators and refocus attention on what the reader needs to know, we make the passage more pointed:

> We must notify every section that uses the storage facility that they must not exceed the prescribed kilogram-per-square-meter floor weight. Tests have established the structural integrity of the transverse beams. They are strong enough to carry the prescribed weights but no more.

Unless your subject matter is the *way* you arrived at your observations or conclusion, you can usually be more concise and direct if you simply present the most salient observations and conclusions, minus the metadiscourse or narrative.

Some writers slip anonymous attribution into their prose by stating that something has been *observed* to exist, is *found* to exist, is *seen, noticed, noted, remarked,* etc.

High divorce rates **have been observed to occur** in parts of the Northeast that **have been determined to have** especially low population densities.

Regular patterns of drought and precipitation **have been found to coincide** with cycles of sunspot activity.

Unless you have some good reason to hedge a bit, leave out the fact that any unspecified observor has observed, found, noticed, or seen something. Just state what the observer observed:

High divorce rates **occur** in parts of the Northeast that **have** especially low population densities.

Regular patterns of drought and precipitation **coincide** with cycles of sunspot activity.

If this seems too flat-footed, drop in a hedge: . . . *apparently coincide.*

Some metadiscourse is so unnecessary that we wonder whether the writer bothered to read over what he or she has written. But just as "belaboring the obvious" may signal a writer who is a novice in a field, so may some cases of metadiscourse. When someone is thoroughly at home in thinking through a problem, she can suppress in her prose the metadiscourse that records her thinking, allowing little or none of the intellectual process to reach the surface of her prose, or at least to remain in the final draft. Look again at that paper written by the first-year law student (p. 121). Not only did he "belabor the obvious" in regard to the knowledge he rehearsed; he made particularly visible the machinery of his thinking (I boldface the metadiscourse and italicize the self-evident):

It is my opinion that the ruling of the lower court concerning the case of HASLEM v. LOCKWOOD should be upheld, *thereby denying the appeal of the plaintiff.* **The main point supporting my point of view on this case concerns** *the tenet of our court system which holds that in order to win his case, the plaintiff must prove that he was somehow wronged by the defendant. The burden of proof rests on the plaintiff. He must show enough evidence to convince the court that he is in the right.*

However, in this case, I do not believe that the plaintiff has satisfied this requirement. In order to prove that the defendant owes him recompense for the six loads of manure, he must first show that he was the legal owner of those loads, and then show that the defendant removed the manure for his own use. **Certainly, there is little doubt as to** the second portion of the evidence; the defendant admits that he did remove the manure to his own land. **Therefore,** the plaintiff must prove the first part of the requirement—**that is,** that he had legal ownership of the manure.

If we deleted all the deadwood from this, all the redundancy, everything that could be inferred by knowledgeable readers, we would be left with something a bit leaner:

> Plaintiff failed to prove he owned the manure. Affirmed.

Again, it is easy to judge this kind of writing as "wordy," but we ought not thereby assume that the writer has an intrinsic problem with his ability to write. Though he may have a problem, he may also be simply at that stage in his writing where he has not yet learned to avoid recording—or later deleting—evidence of his thinking in the way that most experts do.

Not the Negative

For all practical purposes, these two sentences mean about the same thing:

> Don't write in the negative.
> Write in the affirmative.

But if we want to be more concise and direct, we should prefer:

> Write in the affirmative.

To understand many negatives, we have to translate them into affirmatives, because the negative may only imply what we should do by telling us what we shouldn't do. The affirmative states it directly. Compare what you just read with this:

> "Don't write in the negative" and "Write in the affirmative" **do not mean** different things. But if **we don't want** to be indirect, then we **should not prefer** "Don't write in the negative." **We don't have to translate** an affirmative statement **in order not to misunderstand** it because it **does not imply** what we should do.

We can't translate every negative into an affirmative. But we can rephrase many. Some negatives allow almost formulaic translations into affirmatives:

not many → few
not the same → different
not different → alike/similar
did not → failed to
does not have → lacks
did not stay → left
not old enough → too young
did not remember → forgot
did not consider → ignored
did not allow → prevented
did not accept → rejected
not clearly → unclearly
not possible → impossible
not able → unable
not certain → uncertain

Now certainly this advice does not apply to those sentences that raise an issue by contradicting or denying some point that we intend to correct (as this sentence demonstrates). One of the most common ways we introduce discourse is to deny, to say "not so" to someone else's idea of the truth, or even some possible truth. Once we deny it, we then go on to assert the truth as we see it:

> In the last decade of the 20th century, we will not find within our own borders sufficient oil to meet our needs, nor will we find it in the world market. The only way we will increase our oil supply is by developing the one resource that we have so far ignored: massive conservation.

When you combine negatives with passives, nominalizations, and compounds in sentences that are already a bit complex, your writing can become opaque:

> Disengagement of the gears is not possible without locking mechanism release.

> Payments should not be forwarded if there has not been due notification of this office.

These negatives involve two events, one a precondition of the other. We can almost always recast such negatives into more direct affirmatives if we change nominalizations into clauses and passives into actives.

> To disengage the gears, first release the locking mechanism.
>
> Before you forward any payments, notify this office.

Which you put first—the outcome or the condition—depends on what the reader already knows, or what the reader is looking for. For example, if you are trying to explain how to reach some known objective, acquire some desired object, put that first:

> Except when applicants have submitted applications without appropriate documentation, **benefits** will not be denied.

In this case, we can assume the reader is looking for benefits. Then we put that first, but in the affirmative:

> You will receive benefits if you submit appropriate documents.

Or:

> To receive benefits, submit appropriate documents.

As you can see from this example, it is especially important to avoid using negatives along with implicitly negative verbs and connecting words such as these:

> **verbs:** preclude, prevent, lack, fail, doubt, reject, avoid; deny, refuse, exclude, contradict, prohibit, bar, etc.
> **conjunctions:** except, unless, provided, however; without, against, lacking, absent, but for.

One almost formulaic translation involves the words *unless, except,* and *without,* three favorite words when we want to stipulate conditions to an action. We often put the conditional action in the negative, and then introduce the conditions that make the action possible with *unless, without,* or *except:*

> **No** provision of this agreement will be waived **unless** done in writing by either party.

The action that is conditioned is a waiver. While we might want to emphasize the importance of *not* doing something, we are ordinarily more concerned about how *to* do something. So we ought to express that action in the affirmative:

> If either party wishes to waive any provision of this agreement, he must do so in writing.

The translation almost always works:

> X may not do Y unless/except/without doing Z.
> → X may do Y only if X does Z.
> → In order to do Y, X must do Z.

Sentences in their variety run from simplicity to complexity, a progression not necessarily reflected in length: a long sentence may be extremely simple in construction—indeed must be simple if it is to convey its sense easily.

Sir Herbert Read

A long complicated sentence should force itself upon you, make you know yourself knowing it.

Gertrude Stein

8

Length

The ability to write clear, crisp sentences that never go beyond twenty words is a considerable achievement. You'll never confuse a reader with sprawl, wordiness, or muddy abstraction. But if you never write sentences longer than twenty words, you'll be like a pianist who uses only the middle octave: you can carry the tune, but without much variety or range. Every competent writer has to know how to write a concise sentence and how to prune a long one to readable length. But a competent writer must also know how to manage a long sentence gracefully, how to make it as clear and as vigorous as a series of short ones.

Now, several long clauses in a single sentence do not in themselves constitute formless sprawl. Here is a sentence with eighteen subordinate clauses, seventeen of them leading up to the single main clause and the eighteenth bringing up the end:

> Now if nature should intermit her course and leave altogether, though it were but for a while, the observation of her own laws; if those principal and mother elements of the world, whereof all things in this lower world are made, should lose the qualities which now they have; if the frame of that heavenly arch erected over our heads should loosen and dissolve itself; if celestial spheres should forget their wonted motions, and by irregular volubility turn themselves any way as it might happen; if the prince of the lights of heaven, which now as a giant doth run his unwearied course, should, as it were through a languishing faintness, begin to stand and to rest himself; if the moon should wander from her beaten way, the times and seasons of the year blend themselves by disordered and confused mixture, the winds breathe out their last gasp, the clouds yield no rain, the earth be defeated of heavenly influence, the fruits of the earth pine away as children at the with-

ered breasts of their mother no longer able to yield them relief—
what would become of man himself, whom these things now do
all serve?
—Thomas Hooker, *Of the Laws of Ecclesiastical Polity,* 1594

Whatever else we may want to say about that sentence, it does
not sprawl. Its Ciceronian intricacy may no longer appeal to
most modern ears, but its clauses fit together as neatly as the universe Hooker describes. So it is not length alone, or number of
clauses alone, that we ought to worry about, but rather long sentences without shape.

Here are a few ways to extend a sentence and still keep it clear
and graceful.

Coordination

We can join grammatically equal segments with *and, but, yet*
or *or* anywhere in a sentence. But we do it most gracefully after
the subject, in the predicate. If we create a long subject, our
reader has to hold her breath until she gets to the verb. Compare
the second sentence in each of these two passages. The first is
Gore Vidal's original account of how the Founding Fathers viewed
democracy and monarchy, the other my revision.

> The Inventors of the United States decided that there would
> be no hereditary titles in God's country. Although the Inven-
> tors were hostile to the idea of democracy and believed pro-
> foundly in the sacredness of property and the necessary dignity
> of those who owned it, they did not like the idea of king, duke,
> marquess, earl.

> The Inventors of the United States decided that there would be no
> hereditary titles in God's country. Their profound belief in the
> necessary dignity of those who owned property and in its sacred-
> ness and a hostility to the idea of democracy did not lead them to
> like the idea of king, duke, marquess, and earl.

Vidal designed his coordinations so that they all appeared
after his subject, and ordered them so that the shorter elements
of the coordinations appeared before the longer ones:

Although the Inventors
- were hostile to the idea of democracy

and

- believed profoundly in
  - the sacredness of property

  and

  - the necessary dignity of those who owned it,

they did not like the idea of
- king,
- duke,
- marquess,
- earl.

In general, a vigorous sentence moves quickly from a short and specific subject through a strong verb to its complement, where we can, if we wish, more gracefully elaborate our syntax and more fully develop our ideas. So if we extend a sentence by coordinating its parts, we should coordinate after the subject.

In using coordination to build longer sentences, we have to avoid two problems.

1. *Faulty Parallelism.* When we coordinate sentence parts that have different grammatical structures, we may create an offensive lack of parallelism. A common rule of rhetoric and grammar is that we should coordinate elements only of the same grammatical structure: clause and clause, predicate and predicate, prepositional phrase and prepositional phrase, etc. Most careful writers would avoid this:

These advertisements persuade us
- that the corporation supports environmentalism

  but not
- to buy its frivolous products.

Corrected:

. . . persuade us
- **that the corporation supports** environmentalism

  but not
- **that we should buy** its frivolous products.

This also would be considered nonparallel:

The committee recommends

{

- completely revising the curriculum in applied education in order to reflect trends in local employment

  and

- that the administrative structure of the division be modified to reflect the new curriculum

Corrected:

. . . recommends

{

- that the curriculum in applied education be completely revised in order to reflect trends in local employment

  and

- that the administrative structure of the division be modified to reflect the new curriculum.

And yet, some nonparallel coordinations occur in well-written prose fairly often. Writers frequently join a noun phrase with a *how*-clause.

Every attempt will be made to delineate

{

- the problems of biomedical education among the underdeveloped nations

  and

- how a coordinated effort can address them in the most economical and expeditious way.

Or an adjective or adverb with a prepositional phrase:

The grant proposal appears to have been written

{

- intelligently, carefully,

  and

- with the full cooperation of all the agencies whose interests this project involves.

Some teachers and editors would insist on rewriting these into parallel form:

... to delineate

{ the **problems** of biomedical education

and

the **coordinated effort** necessary for the most economical and expeditious solution. }

The grant proposal appears to have been written with

{ **intelligence,**
care,

and

the **full cooperation of** ... }

But most educated readers don't even notice this "faulty" parallelism, much less find it offensive.

2. *Lost Connections.* What will bother readers more than mildly faulty parallelism is a coordination so long that they either lose track of its internal connections or, worse, misread them:

> Every teacher ought to remind himself daily that his students are vulnerable people, insecure and uncertain about those everyday, ego-bruising moments that adults no longer concern themselves with, and that they do not understand that one day they will become as confident and as secure as the adults that bruise them.

That momentary flicker of hesitation about where to connect

> ... and that they do not understand that one day they ...

is enough to interrupt the flow of the sentence.

To revise a sentence like this, try to shorten the first half of the coordination so that the second half is closer to that point in the sentence where the coordination begins:

> Every teacher ought to remind himself that his students are more vulnerable to those ego-bruising moments that adults have learned to cope with and that those students do not understand that one day ...

If you can't do that, try repeating a word that will remind the reader where the second half of the coordination begins:

Every teacher ought **to remind himself that** his students are vulnerable to those ego-bruising moments that adults have learned to cope with, **to remind himself that** those students do not understand that one day. . . .

And, of course, you can always begin a new sentence:

. . . adults no longer concern themselves with. Teachers should remind themselves that their students do not understand. . . .

Subordination

Resumptive Modifiers

A resumptive modifier is a simple device that lets you extend any sentence almost indefinitely. To create a resumptive modifier, repeat a key word close to the end of a clause and then resume the line of thought with a relative clause, elaborating on what went before. Compare

For several years the Columbia Broadcasting System created and developed situation comedies that were the best that American TV had to offer, such as "The Mary Tyler Moore Show" and "All in the Family" that sparkled with wit and invention.

For several years, the Columbia Broadcasting System created and developed situation **comedies** that were the best that American TV had to offer,
> **comedies** such as "The Mary Tyler Moore Show" and "All in the Family,"
> **comedies** that sparkled with wit and invention.

At best, that first sentence verges on monotony. The writer tacked on a relative clause, *comedies that were the best,* and then without a pause a second, *"All in the Family" that sparkled with wit and invention.* The resumptive modifiers in the revision let us pause for a moment, catch our breath, and then move on.

You can pause and resume with parts of speech other than nouns. Here with adjectives:

It was American writers who first used a vernacular that was both **true** and **lyrical,**
> **true** to the rhythms of the working man's speech,
> **lyrical** in its celebration of the land.

Here with verbs:

Humans have been defined by some as the only animal that can
laugh at grief,
    laugh at the pain and tragedy that define their fate.

Summative Modifiers

Somewhat similar is the *summative modifier*. With a summative modifier, you end a segment of a sentence with a comma,
then sum up in a noun or noun phrase what you have just said,
and then continue with a relative clause. Compare these:

> In the last five years, European population growth has dropped to
> almost zero, **which** in years to come will have profound social
> implications.

> In the last five years, European population growth has dropped to
> almost zero,
>   **a demographic event that** in years to come will have pro-
>   found social implications.

> Scientists have finally unraveled the mysteries of the human gene,
> **which** may lead to the control of such dread diseases as cancer
> and birth defects.

> Scientists have finally unraveled the mysteries of the human gene,
>   **a discovery that** may lead to the control of such dread dis-
>   eases as cancer and birth defects.

The summative modifier avoids the gracelessness and the potential ambiguity of a vague *which* and lets the writer extend the
line of the sentence without slipping into a drone.

In Chapter 2 we mentioned that a clear style did not necessarily mean one ten-word sentence after another. Should you find
that your own writing verges on that kind of monotony, you can
use any of the devices described here to combine a series of short,
choppy sentences into fewer, more flowing ones:

> In 1986, President Reagan proposed that federal and state em-
> ployees voluntarily submit to blood and urine tests for drugs. The
> employees took the U.S. Government to court. They claimed that
> the order violated their Fourth Amendment rights. These rights
> protect us against unreasonable search and seizure. But without
> such programs of massive testing and mandatory treatment, drugs
> will continue to devastate our inner cities. They will also devas-
> tate suburbs and rural communities as well. At that point we will

learn what it is like to live with drug addicts and with violent crime. It is a prospect that should frighten us all.

In 1986, President Reagan proposed that federal and state employees voluntarily submit to blood and urine tests for drugs. The employees took the U.S. Government to court, claiming that the order violated their Fourth Amendment rights, rights that protect us against unreasonable search and seizure. But without such programs of massive testing and mandatory treatment, drugs will continue to devastate not only the inner cities but suburbs and rural communities as well. At that point, we will all realize what it is like to live not only with drug addicts but with violent crime, a prospect that should frighten us all.

Free Modifiers

A third kind of modifier that lets you extend a sentence and still avoid monotony resembles the previous two but works a bit differently. This modifier follows the verb but comments on its subject. It usually makes more specific what you assert in the preceding clause that you attach it to. Compare:

> Socrates, who relentlessly questioned the very foundations of social and political behavior, forced his fellow citizens to examine the duty they owed to the laws of their gods and to the laws of their state and encouraged young people to question the authority of their elders while he maintained that he was only trying in his poor inadequate way to puzzle out the truth as best he could.

> Socrates relentlessly questioned the very foundations of social and political behavior,
>> **forcing** his fellow citizens to examine the duty they owed to the laws of their gods and to the laws of their state,
>>
>> **encouraging** young people to question the authority of their elders,
>>
>> **maintaining** all the while that he was only trying in his poor inadequate way to puzzle out the truth as best he could.

These free modifiers most often begin with an *-ing* participle:

> The Scopes monkey trial was a watershed in American religious thinking,
>> **legitimizing** the contemporary interpretation of the Bible and
>>
>> **making** literal fundamentalism a backwater of anti-intellectual theology.

But they can also begin with a past participle form of the verb:

Leonardo da Vinci was a man of powerful intellect,
    driven by an insatiable curiosity and
    haunted by a vision of artistic expression.

Or with an adjective:

In 1939 the United States began to assist the British in their struggle
against Germany,
    fully aware that it faced another world war.

Movement and Momentum

A well-managed long sentence can be just as clear and crisp as several short ones. A writer who can handle a long sentence gracefully lets us take a breath at reasonable intervals and at appropriate places; one part of the sentence will echo another with coordinated and parallel elements. And if she avoids muddling about in abstraction and weak passives, each sentence will move with the directness and energy that a readable style demands.

But if a sentence is to flow easily, its writer should also avoid making us hesitate over words and phrases that break its major grammatical links—subject-verb, verb-object. We should be able to complete those links quickly and surely. Here, for example, is a sentence that does not flow:

A semantic theory, if it is to represent in real-time terms on-line cognitive behavior, must propose more neurally plausible psychological processes than those described here.

This flows more smoothly:

If a semantic theory is to represent on-line cognitive behavior in real-time terms, it must propose psychological processes more neurally plausible than those described here.

Both sentences make us pause, but the first forces us to hold our breath after the subject, *A semantic theory,* until we reach the verb, *must propose.* And at the same time, when we read the *if*-clause buried in the subject, we also have to suspend the verb, *represent,* until we complete it with *on-line cognitive behavior.* And then the *more* at the end is split from its second member, *than those described here.*

A semantic theory → .... ← must propose
    if it is to represent → .... ← on-line cognitive behavior
                    in real-time terms

must propose → ← neurally plausible psychological processes
        more → .... ← than those described here.

The second sentence lets us take a breath half way through, when we finish the introductory clause. But more important, in both clauses, we are able to connect subjects with verbs and verbs with objects immediately:

If a semantic theory → ← is to represent → ← on-line cognitive behavior → ← in real time terms, it → ← must propose → ← psychological processes → ← more neurally plausible → ← than those suggested here.

Grammatical Connections

In most sentences the normal word order is subject-verb-object. If you delay or muddy the subject-verb connection, your reader may have to hesitate, backtrack, reread looking for it.

It's true that competent writers may interrupt the subject-verb link with phrases and clauses. And it's true that many short adverbs fit between subject and verb quite comfortably:

Scientists the world over **deliberately** write in a style that is aloof, impersonal, and objective.

But longer phrases and clauses fit less comfortably:

Scientists the world over, **because they deliberately write in a style that is aloof, impersonal, and objective,** have difficulty communicating with laypeople.

If nothing else precedes the subject, you lose little by moving a long modifying phrase or clause to the beginning of its sentence:

Because scientists the world over deliberately write in a style that is aloof, impersonal, and objective, they have difficulty communicating with laypeople.

When you place your modifier at the beginning of its sentence, you avoid that flicker of hesitation which, if repeated, can break the flow.

The Smallest Connections

If you want to avoid even the smallest hitch in the rhythm of a sentence, you might look closely for adjectives that have become separated from the phrases that modify them:

The accountant has given *as accurate a* projection *as any that could be provided.*

We are facing *a more serious* decision *than what you described earlier.*

A *close* relationship *to the one just discovered* is the degree to which *similar* genetic material *to that of related species* can be modified by *different* DNA chains *from the ones first selected by Adams and Walsh.*

Another course of action *than the present one* is necessary to accumulate *sufficient* capital *to complete such* projects *as those you have described.*

In each case, the adjective—usually an adjective being compared—is split from its following phrase:

as accurate . . . as any that could be provided
more serious . . . than what
close . . . to the one
similar . . . to that
different . . . from the ones
another . . . than the present
sufficient . . . to complete
such . . . as those you

We can maintain in a smoother rhythm if we put the adjective *after* the noun, next to the phrase that completes the adjective:

The accountant has given a projection *as accurate as any that could have been provided.*

We are facing a decision *more serious than what you described earlier.*

A relationship *close to the one just discovered* is the degree to which genetic material *similar to that of related species* can be modified by DNA chains *different from the ones first selected by Adams and Walsh.*

A course of action *other than the present one is* necessary to accumulate capital *sufficient to complete* projects *such as those you describe.*

Some of the adjectives that we most frequently split off from their modifying phrases are these: *more . . . than, less . . . than, other . . . than, as . . . as, similar . . . to, equal . . . to, identical . . . to, same . . . as, different . . . from, such . . . as, separate . . . from, distant . . . from, related . . . to, close . . . to, next . . . to, difficult . . . to, easy . . . to, necessary . . . to.*

Artful Interruptions

Having emphasized how important it is not to interrupt the flow of a sentence, we should now point out that some accomplished writers do exactly that with considerable effect. In this next passage, the anthropologist Clifford Geertz suspends one grammatical construction after another so that he may insert asides, definitions, qualifications, self-corrections, and fuller specifications:

> To argue (point out, actually, for like aerial perspective or the Pythagorean theorem, the thing once seen cannot then be unseen) that the writing of ethnography involves telling stories, making pictures, concocting symbolisms, and deploying tropes is commonly resisted, often fiercely, because of a confusion, endemic in the West since Plato at least, of the imagined with the imaginary, the fictional with the false, making things out with making them up. The strange idea that reality has an idiom in which it prefers to be described, that its very nature demands we talk about it without fuss—a spade is a spade, a rose is a rose—on pain of illusion, trumpery, and self-bewitchment, leads on to the even stranger idea that, if literalism is lost, so is fact.
> —Clifford Geertz, *Works and Lives: The Anthropologist as Author*[10]

As we read this, we feel we are hearing someone simultaneously thinking thoughts, refining, and recording them. Had Geertz thought less interesting thoughts, his interrupted style might seem merely a distracting mannerism. But we are interested not just in what Geertz thinks, but also, because he is Geertz, in how he thinks. So we interpret this interrupted style not as clumsiness but as the record of an interesting mind at work.

Here is that passage revised according to the principles we've discussed so far. What the passage loses in translation is Geertz.

> We have pointed out that those who write ethnography tell stories, make pictures, concoct symbolisms, and deploy tropes, but

many fiercely resist this because they confuse what we can imagine with what is imaginary, what we fictionalize with what is false, what we can make out with what we can make up. We don't have to argue this point. It is like aerial perspective or the Pythagorean theorem: once we have seen a thing we cannot unsee it. Westerners have confused these distinctions at least since Plato. We could adopt the strange idea that reality prefers us to describe it in a particular idiom, that its very nature demands that we talk about it without fuss: we call a spade a spade, a rose a rose. We assume that if we do not reject the idea that we tell stories, we risk illusion, trumpery, and self-bewitchment. But suppose we do adopt these ideas? Then we are led on to the even stranger idea: if we lose literalism, we also lose fact.

This same interrupted style may also suggest not a mind recorded in the act of thinking, but a mind that has already achieved a thought so nuanced, so complex that the writer cannot state it simple and whole, but must, rather, qualify it in every other phrase:

> By a slow movement whose necessity is hardly perceptible, everything that for at least some twenty centuries tended toward and finally succeeded in being gathered under the name of language is beginning to let itself be transferred to, or at least summarized under, the name of writing. By a hardly perceptible necessity, it seems as though the concept of writing—no longer indicating a particular, derivative, auxiliary form of language in general (whether understood as communication, relation, expression, signification, constitution of meaning or thought, etc.), no longer designating the exterior surface, the insubstantial double of a major signifier, *the signifier of the signifier*—is beginning to go beyond the extension of language.
> —Jacques Derrida, *Of Grammatology*[11]

Principles of style do not exist so that masters of style may ignore them. But it is when a writer does ignore them that we see most clearly how well that writer has mastered her craft.

Problems with Modifiers

When we add several modifiers to a clause, sentences may become confusing because the reader will lose track of the logical and grammatical connections between the modifier and the thing modified.

Dangling Modifiers

A modifier "dangles" when its implied subject differs from the specific subject of the clause that follows it:

In order to contain the epidemic the area was sealed off.

The implied subject of *contain,* some person or agency, is different from the subject of the main clause, *the area.*

Resuming negotiations after a break of several days, the same issues confronted both the union and the company.

The implied subject of *resuming, the union and the company,* is different from the subject of the main clause, *the same issues.*

Constructions like these more often amuse than confuse us. But since they cause some readers to hesitate for a moment, you ought to avoid them on general principles. Either rewrite the introductory phrase so that it has its own subject or make the subject of the main clause agree with the implied subject of the introductory phrase:

In order for **us** to contain the epidemic, the area was sealed off.
In order to contain the epidemic, the **city** sealed off the area.

When **the union and the company** resumed negotiations, the same issues confronted them.
Resuming negotiations after a break of several days, **the union and the company** confronted the same issues.

Some modifiers that seem to dangle are in fact acceptable. If either the modifier or the subject of the main clause is part of the metadiscourse, the modifier will seem entirely appropriate to most readers:

In order to start the motor, **it is essential** that the retroflex cam connecting rod be disengaged.

To summarize, *unemployment* in the southern tier of counties remains the state's major economic and social problem.

Misplaced Modifiers

A second problem with modifiers is that sometimes they seem to modify two things, or the wrong thing. One kind of ambiguous modifier can refer either forward or back:

Overextending oneself in strenuous physical activity **too frequently** results in a variety of physical ailments.

We failed **entirely** to understand the complexities of the problem.

In each of these, the modifier can just as easily appear in an unambiguous position:

Overextending oneself **too frequently** in strenuous exercise. . . .

Overextending oneself in physical exercise results **too frequently** in a variety of physical ailments.

We **entirely** failed to understand. . . .
We failed to understand **entirely**. . . .

A second ambiguity occurs when a modifier at the end of a clause or sentence can modify either a neighboring or a more distant phrase:

Scientists have learned that their observations are as necessarily subjective as those in any other field **in recent years**.

We can move the modifier to a less ambiguous position:

In recent years, scientists have learned that. . . .
Scientists have learned that **in recent years**, their observations. . . .

In these cases, we can also use a resumptive modifier to clarify what a modifier is supposed to modify. In the next sentence, for example, what is it that dictates—the relationships, the components, or the process?

Perhaps there are relationships among the components of the process that would dictate one order rather than another.

A moment's thought suggests that the relationships dictate, but why should we cause our reader to pause even for a moment to understand how one idea connects to another? A resumptive modifier would make it clear:

Perhaps there are relationships among the components of the process, **relationships** that would dictate one order rather than another.

Pronoun Reference

A long sentence can also create problems with pronoun reference. If there is the slightest chance that a pronoun will confuse your reader, don't hesitate to repeat the antecedent. And if you can conveniently make one of your nouns plural and another singular, you can use singular and plural pronouns to distinguish what you're referring to.

Compare these:

> **Physicians** must never forget that **their patients** are vitally concerned about **their** treatment and **their** prognosis, but that **they** are often unwilling to ask for fear of what **they** will say.

> **A physician** must never forget that **her patients** are vitally concerned about **their** treatment and **their** prognosis, but that **they** are often unwilling to ask for fear of what **she** will say.

Anything is better than not to write clearly. There is nothing to be said against lucidity, and against simplicity only the possibility of dryness. This is a risk well worth taking when you reflect how much better it is to be bald than to wear a curly wig.

Somerset Maugham

But clarity and brevity, though a good beginning, are only a beginning. By themselves, they may remain bare and bleak. When Calvin Coolidge, asked by his wife what the preacher had preached on, replied "Sin," and, asked what the preacher had said, replied "He was against it," he was brief enough. But one hardly envies Mrs. Coolidge.

F. L. Lucas

There are two sorts of eloquence; the one indeed scarce deserves the name of it, which consists chiefly in laboured and polished periods, an over-curious and artificial arrangement of figures, tinselled over with a gaudy embellishment of words, . . . The other sort of eloquence is quite the reverse to this, and which may be said to be the true characteristic of the holy Scriptures; where the eloquence does not arise from a laboured and far-fetched elocution, but from a surprising mixture of simplicity and majesty, . . .

Laurence Sterne

In literature the ambition of the novice is to acquire the literary language; the struggle of the adept is to get rid of it.

G. B. Shaw

9

Elegance

Let's assume that you can now write clear, coherent, and appropriately emphatic prose. That in itself would constitute a style of such singular distinction that most of us would be satisfied to have achieved so much. But though we might prefer bald clarity to the turgidity of most institutional prose, the relentless simplicity of the plain style can finally become flat and dry, eventually arid. Its plainness invests prose with the virtuous blandness of unsalted meat and potatoes—honest fare to be sure, but hardly memorable and certainly without zest. Sometimes a touch of class, a flash of elegance, can mark the difference between forgettable Spartan prose and an idea so elegantly expressed that it fixes itself in the mind of your reader.

Now, I can't tell you how to be graceful and elegant in the same way I can tell you how to be clear and direct. What I *can* do is describe a few of the devices that some graceful writers use. But that advice is, finally, about as useful as listing the ingredients in the bouillabaisse of a great cook and then expecting anyone to make it. Knowing the ingredients and knowing how to use them is the difference between reading cookbooks and Cooking.

What follows describes a few ingredients of a modestly elegant style. How imaginatively and skillfully you use them is the difference between reading this book on writing, and Writing.

Balance and Symmetry

We've already described how you can use coordination to extend a sentence beyond a few words. Coordination itself will grace a sentence with a movement more rhythmic and satisfying than that of most noncoordinate sentences. Compare the styles of these two versions of Walter Lippmann's argument about the need for a balance of powers in a democratic society.

The national unity of a free people depends upon a sufficiently even balance of political power to make it impracticable for the administration to be arbitrary and for the opposition to be revolutionary and irreconcilable. Where that balance no longer exists, democracy perishes. For unless all the citizens of a state are forced by circumstances to compromise, unless they feel that they can affect policy but that no one can wholly dominate it, unless by habit and necessity they have to give and take, freedom cannot be maintained.

The national unity of a free people depends upon a sufficiently even balance of political power to make it impracticable for there to be an arbitrary administration against a revolutionary opposition that is irreconcilably opposed to it. Where that balance no longer exists, democracy perishes. For unless all the citizens of a state are habitually forced by necessary circumstances to compromise in a way that lets them affect policy with no one dominating it, freedom cannot be maintained.

In my version, the sentences just run on from one phrase to the next, from one clause to another. In his version, Lippmann balances phrase against phrase, clause against clause, creating an architectural symmetry that supports the whole passage. We can see more clearly how his sentences work if we break them out into their parts.

The national unity of a free people depends upon a sufficiently even balance of political power to make it impracticable

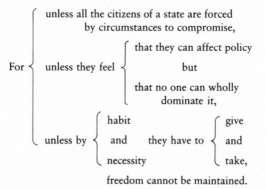

for the administration to be arbitrary

and

for the opposition to be ⟨ revolutionary and irreconcilable.

Where that balance no longer exists, democracy perishes.

For ⟨ unless all the citizens of a state are forced by circumstances to compromise,

unless they feel ⟨ that they can affect policy but that no one can wholly dominate it,

unless by ⟨ habit and necessity ⟩ they have to ⟨ give and take,

freedom cannot be maintained.

We can enhance the rhythm and grace of coordination if we keep in mind a few simple principles. First, a coordinate series will move more gracefully if each succeeding coordinate element is longer than the one before it. So if you coordinate within a coordination, do it in the last branch of the main coordination.

We can use correlative conjunctions such as *both X and Y, not only X but also Y, neither X nor Y* to signify a balanced coordination and give it emphasis. Compare these:

The national significance of an ethnic minority depends upon a sufficiently deep historical identity that makes it

- impossible for the majority to absorb the minority
- and
- inevitable that the minority will
  - maintain its identity
  - and
  - transmit its heritage.

The national significance of an ethnic minority depends upon a sufficiently deep historical identity that makes it

- **not only** impossible for the majority to absorb the minority
- **but**
- inevitable that the minority will
  - **both** maintain its identity
  - **and**
  - transmit its heritage.

The second is stronger than the first.

You can make these coordinate patterns more rhetorically elegant if you consciously balance parts of phrases and clauses against each other:

Neither
- the vacuous emotion of daytime soap opera
- nor
- the mindless eroticism of nighttime sitcoms

reflects the best
- that American artists are able to create
- or
- that American audiences are willing to support.

The richest kind of balance and parallelism counterpoints both grammar and meaning: here *vacuous* is balanced against *mindless, emotion* against *eroticism, daytime* against *nighttime, soap opera* against *sitcoms, artists* against *audiences, able* against *willing,* and *create* against *support.*

You can achieve the same effect when you balance parts of sentences that are not coordinated. Here is a subject balanced against an object. (The square brackets signal a balanced but not coordinate pair.)

> ⌈ Scientists who tear down established views of universe invariably
> challenge
> ⌊ those of us who have built all our visions of reality on those views.

Here, the predicate of a relative clause in a subject is balanced against the predicate of the whole sentence.

> A government that is unwilling to
> ⌈ listen to the moderate voices of its citizenry
> ⌊ must eventually answer to the harsh justice of its revolutionaries.

A direct object balanced against the object of a preposition:

> Those of us who are vitally concerned about our failing school systems are not quite ready to sacrifice
> ⌈ the intellectual growth of our innocent children
>
>   to
>
> ⌊ the social daydreaming of irresponsible bureaucrats.

Here is an introductory subordinate clause (1a) balanced against a main clause (1b), the object of that subordinate clause (2a) balanced against the object in a following prepositional phrase (2b), and the object of the main clause (3a) balanced against the objects in two following prepositional phrases (3b–c).

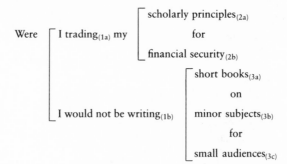

None of these are coordinated, but they are all consciously balanced. Like every other artful device, these balanced phrases and clauses can eventually become self-defeating—or at least monotonously arch. But if you use them unobtrusively when you want to emphasize an important point or conclude the line of an argument, you can give your prose a shape and a cadence that most ordinary writing lacks.

Emphasis and Rhythm

As we have seen, emphasis is largely a matter of controlling the way a sentence ends. When we maneuver our most important information into that stressed position, the natural emphasis we hear in our mind's ear underscores the rhetorical emphasis of a significant idea. But the sentence will still seem weak and anticlimactic if it ends with lightweight words.

Different parts of speech carry different weights. Prepositions are very light—one reason why we sometimes avoid leaving a preposition at the end. Sentences should move toward strength; a preposition can dilute that strength. Compare:

> The intellectual differences among races is a subject that only the most politically indifferent scientist *is willing to look into.*

> The intellectual differences among races is a subject that only the most politically indifferent scientist *is willing to explore.*

Adjectives and adverbs are heavier than prepositions, but lighter than verbs and nouns. The heaviest, the most emphatic words are nominalizations, those abstract nouns that in Chapter 2 we worked so hard to eliminate. But we worked hard to eliminate them mostly at the beginnings of sentences, where you want to get off to a brisk start. When you end a sentence with a nominalization, you create a different effect. You bring the sentence to an end with a climactic thump.

Compare these two versions of Winston Churchill's "Finest Hour" speech, in which Churchill, always an elegant and emphatic writer, ends with the elegant parallelism emphasized by the pair of nominalizations:

> . . . until in God's good time, the New World, with all its power and might, steps forth to the **rescue** and the **liberation** of the old.

He could have written more simply, more directly, and much more banally:

> . . . until in God's good time, the powerful New World steps forth to liberate the old.

In this next passage, E. B. White was writing about a rather less dramatic event, the death of a favorite pig. But White wanted to elevate the scene to one approaching mock tragedy, so he drew on the same stylistic resources that Churchill used:

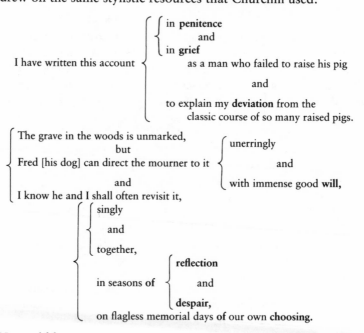

He could have written,

> As a man who failed to raise his pig, I have grieved as I have written this account in order to explain why I deviated from the classic course of so many raised pigs. Although the grave in the woods is unmarked, Fred can unerringly direct the mourner to it with good will. I know the two of us shall often revisit it, at those times when we are reflecting on things and when we are despairing, on flagless memorial days that we shall choose.

But without the elegant touches, without the parallelisms and the emphatic final nominalizations, the passage becomes merely silly.

Here is a passage by the political scientist and statesman, George Kennan. He describes Averell Harriman, an American diplomat working in the Soviet Union during World War II, a man of great intelligence and formal elegance. Following it is a version that excludes almost all nominalizations. Which better reflects Harriman's style is obvious:

> Unique in his single-mindedness of purpose, it was his nature to pursue only one interest at a time. When we were associated with each other in Moscow this interest was, properly and commendably, the prospering of the American war effort and American diplomacy, as President Roosevelt viewed and understood it. To the accomplishment of his part in the furtherance of this objective he addressed himself with a dedication, a persistence, and an unflagging energy and attention that has no parallel in my experience. He recognized no interest outside his work. Personal interest did not exist for him. His physical frame, spare and sometimes ailing, seemed at best an unwelcome irrelevance; I had the impression that it was with an angry impatience that he took cognizance of the occasional reminders of its existence, dragged it with him on his daily rounds of duty, and forced it to support him where continuation without its support was not possible.
> —George F. Kennan, *Memoirs: 1925–1950*,[12]

> He was uniquely single-minded; by nature, he pursued only one interest at a time. When we were associated with each other in Moscow, he properly and commendably wanted only to help the American war effort and American diplomatic affairs as President Roosevelt viewed and understood them. To further this objective, he was persistent and dedicated. He had unflagging energy and was attentive to details in a way that parallels nothing I have experienced. He was not interested in anything personal. His physical frame, spare and sometimes ailing, seemed at best something unwelcome and irrelevant. It seemed to me that he was angry and impatient when he recognized those times that it reminded him it existed, when he dragged it with him on his daily round of duty and forced it to support him where he could not have continued without it.

Now, when a writer combines nominalizations with balanced and parallel constructions, when he draws on resumptive and summative modifiers to extend the line of a sentence, we know he is cranking up a style that aims at elegant complexity. This sentence by Frederick Jackson Turner, from his *The Frontier in*

American History, displays most of those devices, plus one more. If you seek an extravagantly elegant style, construct elaborately balanced units, sprinkle them with nominalizations, and then— this will sound odd—end clauses with phrases introduced by *of:* "This then is the heritage **of pioneer experience—**."

> This then is the heritage of pioneer experience—a passionate belief that a democracy was possible which should leave the individual a part to play in free society and not make him a cog in a machine operated from above; which trusted in the common man, in his tolerance, his ability to adjust differences with good humor, and to work out an American type from the contributions of all nations—a type for which he would fight against those who challenged it in arms, and for which in time of war he would make sacrifices, even the temporary sacrifice of individual freedom and his life, lest that freedom be lost forever.

This then is the heritage **of pioneer experience,—**
[free modifier] a passionate belief that a democracy was possible

which should
- leave the individual a part to play in free society

  and

- not make him a cog in a machine operated from above;

which trusted
- in   the common man,

  in
  - his tolerance,

  - his ability to work *an American type* from the contributions of all nations—

[resumptive modifier]
a type
- for which he would fight against those who challenged it in arms,

  and

- for which in time of war he would make *sacrifices,*

[resumptive modifier]
even *the temporary sacrifice* of his
- **individual freedom**

  and

- **life,**

lest that freedom be lost forever.

Length and Rhythm

In ordinary prose, the length of your sentences becomes an issue only if they are all about fifteen words long or if they are all much longer, over thirty or so. Though one eighteen-to-twenty-word sentence after another isn't the ideal goal, they will seem less monotonous than a series of sentences that are regularly longer or shorter.

In artful prose, on the other hand, length is more deliberately controlled. Some accomplished stylists can write one short sentence after another, perhaps to strike a note of urgency:

> Toward noon Petrograd again became the field of military action; rifles and machine guns rang out everywhere. It was not easy to tell who was shooting or where. One thing was clear; the past and the future were exchanging shots. There was much casual firing; young boys were shooting off revolvers unexpectedly acquired. The arsenal was wrecked. . . . Shots rang out on both sides. But the board fence stood in the way, dividing the soldiers from the revolution. The attackers decided to break down the fence. They broke down part of it and set fire to the rest. About twenty barracks came into view. The bicyclists were concentrated in two or three of them. The empty barracks were set fire to at once.
> —Leon Trotsky, *The Russian Revolution*, trans. Max Eastman

Or terse certainty:

> The teacher or lecturer is a danger. He very seldom recognizes his nature or his position. The lecturer is a man who must talk for an hour. France may possibly have acquired the intellectual leadership of Europe when their academic period was cut down to forty minutes. I also have lectured. The lecturer's first problem is to have enough words to fill forty or sixty minutes. The professor is paid for his time, his results are almost impossible to estimate. . . . No teacher has ever failed from ignorance. That is empiric professional knowledge. Teachers fail because they cannot "handle the class." Real education must ultimately be limited to men who IN-SIST on knowing, the rest is mere sheep-herding.
> —Ezra Pound, *ABC of Reading*

Or fire:

> Let us look at this American artist first. How did he ever get to America, to start with? Why isn't he a European still, like his father before him?

Now listen to me, don't listen to him. He'll tell you the lie you expect. Which is partly your fault for expecting it.

He didn't come in search of freedom of worship. England had more freedom of worship in the year 1700 than America had. Won by Englishmen who wanted freedom and so stopped at home and fought for it. And got it. Freedom of worship? Read the history of New England during the first century of its existence.

Freedom anyhow? The land of the free! This the land of the free! Why, if I say anything that displeases them, the free mob will lynch me, and that's my freedom. Free? Why I have never been in any country where the individual has such an abject fear of his fellow countrymen. Because, as I say, they are free to lynch him the moment he shows he is not one of them. . . .

All right then, what did they come for? For lots of reasons. Perhaps least of all in search of freedom of any sort: positive freedom, that is.

—D. H. Lawrence, *Studies in Classic American Literature*

In this last example, Lawrence invests his discourse with even more urgency by breaking sentences into fragments and what could be longer paragraphs into abrupt snatches of discourse.

Equally accomplished writers write one long sentence after another to suggest a mind exploring an idea in the act of writing the sentence:

In any event, up at the front of this March, in the first line, back of that hollow square of monitors, Mailer and Lowell walked in this barrage of cameras, helicopters, TV cars, monitors, loudspeakers, and wavering buckling twisting line of notables, arms linked (line twisting so much that at times the movement was in file, one arm locked ahead, one behind, then the line would undulate about and the other arm would be ahead) speeding up a few steps, slowing down while a great happiness came back into the day as if finally one stood under some mythical arch in the great vault of history, helicoptors buzzing about, chop-chop, and the sense of America divided on this day now liberated some undiscovered patriotism in Mailer so that he felt a sharp searing love for his country in this moment and on this day, crossing some divide in his own mind wider than the Potomac, a love so lacerated he felt as if a marriage were being torn and children lost—never does one love so much as then, obviously, then—and an odor of wood smoke, from where you knew not, was also in the air, a smoke of dignity and some calm heroism, not unlike the sense of freedom which also comes when a marriage is burst—Mailer knew for the

first time why men in the front line of battle are almost always ready to die; there is a promise of some swift transit. . . .
—Norman Mailer, *Armies of the Night*

This single sentence goes on for several hundred more words.

Metaphor

Clarity, vigor, symmetry, rhythm—prose so graced would more than satisfy most of us. And yet, if it offered no virtues other than these, such prose would excite an admiration only for our craft, not for the reach of our imagination. This next passage displays all the stylistic graces we've described, but it goes beyond mere craft. It reveals a truth about pleasure through a figure of speech embedded in a comparison that is itself almost metaphorical.

> The secret of the enjoyment of pleasure is to know when to stop. . . . We do this every time we listen to music. We do not seize hold of a particular chord or phrase and shout at the orchestra to go on playing it for the rest of the evening; on the contrary, however much we may like that particular moment of music, we know that its perpetuation would interrupt and kill the movement of the melody. We understand that the beauty of a symphony is less in these musical moments than in the whole movement from beginning to end. If the symphony tries to go on too long, if at a certain point the composer exhausts his creative ability and tries to carry on just for the sake of filling in the required space of time, then we begin to fidget in our chairs, feeling that he has denied the natural rhythm, has broken the smooth curve from birth to death, and that though a pretense of life is being made, it is in fact a living death.
> —Alan W. Watts, *The Meaning of Happiness*

Watts could have written this:

> . . . however much we may like that particular moment of music, we know that its perpetuation would interrupt and spoil the movement of the melody . . . we begin to fidget in our chairs, feeling that he has denied the natural rhythm, has interrupted the regular movement from beginning to end, and that though a pretense of wholeness is being made, it is in fact a repeated end.

The two passages are equally clear and graceful. But the first illuminates music—and pleasure—in a way that the second does not. The metaphor of birth and the smooth, unbroken curve of life into death startles us with a flash of unexpected truth.

Of metaphor, Aristotle wrote,

> By far the greatest thing is to be a master of metaphor. It is the one thing that cannot be learned from others. It is a sign of genius, for a good metaphor implies an intuitive perception of similarity among dissimilars.

A metaphor invites us to look at two things in a new way. Similes do the same, but less intensely, the *like* or *as* moderating the force of the comparison.

Compare these:

> The schoolmaster is the person who takes the children off the parents' hands for a consideration. That is to say, he establishes a child prison, engages a number of employee schoolmasters as turnkeys, and covers up the essential cruelty and unnaturalness of the situation by torturing the children if they do not learn, and calling this process, which is within the capacity of any fool or blackguard, by the sacred name of Teaching.
> —G. B. Shaw, *Sham Education*

> . . . he establishes something like a child prison, engages a number of employee schoolmasters to act like turnkeys, covers up the essential cruelty and unnaturalness of the situation by doing things to the children that are like torture if they do not learn . . . calling this process, which is within the capacity of any fool or blackguard, by the sacred name of Teaching.

Both passages say the same thing about education, but the first with more intensity and immediacy.

You may think that metaphor is appropriate only to poetic writing, or reflective or polemical writing. But metaphor vivifies all kinds of prose. Historians rely on it:

> This is what may be called the common-sense view of history. History consists of a corpus of ascertained facts. The facts are available to the historian in documents, inscriptions, and so on, like fish on the fishmonger's slab. The historian collects them, takes them home, and cooks and serves them in whatever style appeals to him. Acton, whose culinary tastes were austere, wanted them served plain. . . . Sir George Clark, critical as he was of Acton's attitude, himself contrasts the "hard core of facts" in history

with the "surrounding pulp of disputable interpretation"—forgetting perhaps that the pulpy part of the fruit is more rewarding than the hard core.
—E. H. Carr, *What Is History?*

So do biologists:

Some of you may have been thinking that, instead of delivering a scientific address, I have been indulging in a flight of fancy. It is a flight, but not of mere fancy, nor is it just an individual indulgence. It is my small personal attempt to share in the flight of the mind into new realms of our cosmic environment. We have evolved wings for such flights, in the shape of the disciplined scientific imagination. Support for those wings is provided by the atmosphere of knowledge created by human science and learning: so far as this supporting atmosphere extends, so far can our wings take us in our exploration.
—Julian Huxley, "New Bottles for Old Wine," *Journal of the Royal Anthropological Institute*

And philosophers:

Quine has long professed his skepticism about the possibility of making any sense of the refractory idioms of intentionality, so he needs opacity only to provide a quarantine barrier protecting the healthy, extensional part of a sentence from the infected part.
—Daniel C. Dennett, "Beyond Belief" [13]

And when they are writing of new ideas for which there is yet no standard language, so do physicists:

Whereas the lepton pair has a positive rest mass when it is regarded as a single particle moving with a velocity equal to the vector sum of the motions of its two components, a photon always has zero rest mass. This difference can be glossed over, however, by treating the lepton pair as the offspring of the decay of a short-lived photonlike parent called a virtual photon.
—Leon M. Lederman, "The Upsilon Particle," *Scientific American*

These metaphors serve different ends. Shaw used the prison metaphor to emphasize a point that he could have made without it. But prisons, turnkeys, and torture invest his argument with an emotional intensity that ordinary language could not communicate. Carr used fish and fruit both to emphasize and to illuminate. He could have expressed his ideas more prosaically, but the literal statement would have been longer and weaker. Dennett and Lederman used their comparisons not to emphasize but entirely to explain; neither required any dramatically heightened emphasis.

But if metaphor can sometimes evidence a fresh imagination, it can also betray those of us whose imaginations fall short of its demands. Too often, we use metaphor to gloss over inexact thinking:

> Societies give birth to new values through the differential osmotic flow of daily social interaction. Conflicts evolve when new values collide with the old, a process that frequently spawns yet a new set of values that synthesize the conflict into a reconciliation of opposites.

We get the picture, but through a cracked glass of careless metaphor. The birth metaphor suggests a traumatic event, but the new values, it is claimed, result from osmotic flow, a process constituted by a multitude of invisibly small events. Conflicts do not usually "evolve"; they more often occur in an instant, as suggested by the metaphor of collision. The spawning image picks up the metaphor of birth again, but by this time the image is, at best, collectively ludicrous.

Had the writer thought through his ideas carefully, he might have expressed them in clearer, nonfigurative language:

> As we continuously interact with one another in small ways, we gradually create new social values. When one person behaves according to one of these new values and another according to an old value, the values may come into conflict, creating a new third value that reconciles the other two.

Less misleading, but more embarrassing, are those passages that confuse emphasis with extravagance. Huxley's passage about the wings of inquiry flapping in an atmosphere of scientific knowledge comes perilously close.

Metaphors also invite trouble if we aren't sensitive to the way their literal meanings can unexpectedly intrude. The following is not a concocted example; it actually appeared in a student paper.

> The classic blitzkrieg relies on a tank-heavy offensive force, supported by ground-support aircraft, to destroy the defender's ability to fight by running amuck [*sic*] in his undefended rear, after penetrating his forward defenses.

God does not much mind bad grammar, but He does not take any particular pleasure in it.

Erasmus

It is not the business of grammar, as some critics seem preposterously to imagine, to give law to the fashions which regulate our speech. On the contrary, from its conformity to these, and from that alone, it derives all its authority and value.

George Campbell

No grammatical rules have sufficient authority to control the firm and established usage of language. Established custom, in speaking and writing, is the standard to which we must at last resort for determining every controverted point in language and style.

Hugh Blair

English usage is sometimes more than mere taste, judgment, and education—sometimes it's sheer luck, like getting across the street.

E. B. White

10

Usage

Style, Grammar, and Choice

So far, we've been discussing choice: From among sentences that express the same idea, how do we pick the one that expresses it best? We might prefer (1a) to (1b):

(1a) The comptroller did not support our research sufficiently.

(1b) There was an insufficiency of comptroller research support for us.

But we would not say that (1b) was grammatically wrong, only less direct than it might be.

At first glance, good grammar and appropriate usage seem different. When the *American Heritage Dictionary* says that *irregardless* is "nonstandard . . . never acceptable" (except when we're trying to be humorous), choosing between *irregardless* and *regardless* seems at best academic. It is not a choice between better and worse, but of right and irredeemably, unequivocally wrong.

That simplifies the matter: correct usage does not require good taste or sound judgment, only a reliable memory. If we remember that *irregardless* is always and everywhere wrong, the possibility of choosing it ought never even rise to a level of consciousness. The same would seem to be true for a dozen other "rules":

Don't begin a sentence with *and* or *but.*
Don't end a sentence with a preposition.
Don't split infinitives.
Don't use double negatives.

Unfortunately, questions of "good" grammar are not so easily settled: Many of the grammatical rules that some among us like to invoke are not linguistic fact, but classroom folklore, invented by eighteenth-century grammarians out of whole cloth, repeated by editors unwilling to determine whether those rules comport with reality, taught by teachers who teach what textbooks tell them, and ignored by the best writers everywhere. Other rules of usage are imperatives that we violate at the risk of seeming at least careless, at worst illiterate. These rules are observed by even the less-than-best writers. Then there are rules that we may observe or not, depending first on the effect that we want, then on our confidence to ignore them.

While we might generally agree on what counts as clear and why clarity is important, not all of us will agree on what counts as correct. We can agree about matters of clarity because most of us read in about the same way—so long as we also have roughly the same level of knowledge about a subject. But how we think about correctness depends on our social and geographical origins, on our educational history, even on our character. Moreover, we are a people for whom "good English" is socially important; for many, it is more important than clarity. It is a matter that evokes in some critics a passion so deep that they seem to lose touch with reality. John Simon, a Pop-Grammarian, has claimed,

> The English language is being treated nowadays exactly as slave traders once handled the merchandise in their slave ships, or as the inmates of concentration camps were dealt with by their Nazi jailers.

What linguistic sin could elicit this unusually tasteless and insensitive comparison? The phrase "fellow colleagues," a redundancy, to be sure, but scarcely, as Simon put it, "the rock bottom of linguistic ineptitude" (*Paradigms Lost,* Clarkson N. Potter, Inc., 1980, p. 97). If you have now or think that one day you will have responsibility for the language of others, you must be able to think about correctness in ways more sensible than this.

Two Views of Grammatical Regulation

To some critics, standard written English is just one more device by which those who manage our society exercise their discriminatory and repressive impulses: a standard grammar keeps the underclasses under. To others, standard English is the product of centuries of thoughtful sifting and winnowing, a kind of managed linguistic Darwinism whose results have been formalized by grammarians in rules now observed by the best writers everywhere. Both views are right—trivially and incompletely.

The radical critics are right that what we call standard written English is close to the dialect of most of those who create, manage, and control our schools, our political institutions, and our media of communication, certainly closer than to the dialect of those who are often excluded by them. It is not surprising that those who control those institutions should privilege their own language, because if they did not learn that language at home, they learned it in those same institutions they now control.

And the conservative critics are right that many of the features by which we define Standard English originated in economies of expression and efficiency of communication, and so on those grounds would seem to be naturally privileged. We no longer need an elaborate array of verb endings, and so we no longer use a present tense ending in five out of six contexts: *I /we/you/ you/they leave;* we use a present-tense inflection—anachronistically, perhaps—only in the sixth context, after a singular third person: *She/he/it leaves.*

But both the radical and the conservative views are in more important ways profoundly wrong. Standard written English is not a device invented and maintained to preserve for those who control it their social status and economic privilege. In fact, a standard written language eliminates a major occasion for a prejudice that has afflicted large numbers of societies—the discrimination that results when someone finds an advantage in denigrating the dialect of another. Long before we had a standard English, Englishmen were abusing one another's language. William of Malmesbury (1095–1143), a monk from the south of England, observed that the language of the north was so crude that Englishmen in the south could not understand it. To achieve socially vicious ends, some will discriminate on the basis of any difference, linguistic or otherwise—dress, haircut, table manners, or ZIP code. Only the historically ignorant argue that, since some have used standard English as a device to discriminate against others, it is for just that purpose that standard written English is now taught in our schools.

On the other hand, conservative critics are wrong when they claim that the forms of standard written English constitute by their very nature the best of all possible forms of English. To be sure, many of the features of modern standard English have resulted from linguistic changes that seem to arise from an impulse toward economy and efficiency, and so they now seem desirable. But far from distinguishing standard English from nonstandard English, those features are shared by all speakers of all dialects, regardless of social class or geographical origin. For example, historical evolution has eliminated from all dialects of English many of its irregular verbs. There may be a few isolated rural areas where older speakers still use *holp* and *clum* for *helped* and *climbed,* but no group of younger speakers outside those areas, no matter how uneducated, still do. If regular verbs are better than irregular verbs, then it is a good in which every speaker of every dialect shares. Indeed, the first person who regularized *holp* into *helped* committed at that moment a grammatical error no better than the first person who regularized *go* into *goed.*

Many of those points of grammar that the conservative critics seem most strenuously to condemn as vulgar reflect the undeniable logic of the "uneducated." When someone says, "I'm here, ain't I?" that person uses a wholly logical contraction of *am* + *not; I am here, am* + *not* [→ *ain't*] *I?* What is illogical (i.e., idiosyncratic, irregular, unpredictable) is the "correct" form—*I'm here, aren't I?*, because it derives from a wholly "ungrammatical" *I am here, are* + *not* [→ *aren't*] *I?* Just as *hoped* is more logical than *holp,* so *knowed* is more "logical" than *knew, runned* more logical than *ran.* Since we use possessive pronouns in *my*self, *our*selves, *your*self, *your*selves, *her*self, and *its*[s]elf, it would be "logical" to use the same possessive pronoun in *hisself* and *their*selves. We could point to a dozen other examples where principles of "logic" and "efficiency" should have given us not our currently "correct" form, the form that is the exception to a general principle, but rather the widely condemned "incorrect" form, the form that in fact reflects a mind accurately generalizing from a principle of regularity.

Do not misunderstand me: Regularity or predictability does not make a form socially acceptable. *Hisself, knowed,* and *ain't* remain beyond the linguistic pale. My point is not to make nonstandard English socially acceptable; that would be a hopeless task. My point, rather, is that we ought to rethink the widely shared notion that every feature of standard English has some kind of self-evident, naturally determined "logic" that makes it intrinsically superior to its corresponding form in nonstandard English. In educated written English intended for general circulation, *ain't* is socially "wrong." But we ought not try to convince ourselves or anyone else that *ain't*—along with most other errors of its kind—is wrong because it is inherently defective and is therefore evidence of an inherently defective mind. Such errors are "wrong" because of historically accidental reasons. Until we recognize the arbitrary nature of our judgments, too many of us will take "bad" grammar as evidence of laziness, carelessness, or a low IQ. That belief is not just wrong. It is socially destructive.

A Brief History of Good English

Social distinctions between kinds of English have existed since the beginnings of English society. Twelve centuries ago, even before our forebears called themselves *englisc,* they distinguished its social varieties. In the eighth century, the Venerable Bede (672?–735), an Anglo-Saxon historian, wrote about Imma, a Northumbrian thane of the late seventh century who, after defeat in battle, tried to pass himself off as a simple foot soldier. But even though his captors spoke Mercian, a dialect of Old English different from Northumbrian, they nevertheless recognized his superior social standing because he could not disguise his upper-class demeanor and speech.

In 1066, the Norman Invasion changed what counted as upper-class speech for the next two centuries. Until about the last third of the twelfth century, the prestige language was Anglo-Norman French, and after that the French of Paris. But by the middle of the twelfth century, John of Salisbury observed that it was fashionable to use French words in English conversation, a comment that suggests that at least some English conversations were more fashionable than others.

By the late fourteenth century, English had become the spoken language of choice, even among the upper class. And at the same time, those few who thought about such matters began to distinguish prestige dialects among the different dialects of English. They first distinguished forms of English simply on the basis of geography. Since the English court was located near London, Southern English became more prestigious than Northern. As a result, any dialect of English merely different from Southern became an object of abuse (I have translated this passage into something closer to modern English):

> The language of the Northumbrians, especially at York, is so shrill, cutting, rough, and ill-shaped that we southern men can barely understand it. I believe that is because they are near to foreign men and nations that speak roughly [Higden may have had in mind the Danes, who had invaded and settled the northeastern part of England in the ninth century] and also because the kings of England always live far from that country, for they are more attracted to the south. . . . They are more in the south than in the north because the south may have better grain land, more people, more noble cities, and more profitable harbors.
> —Ranulph Higden, *Polychronicon*, ca. 1380

The first written form of early modern English that could be called standard began to develop in the late fourteenth and early fifteenth centuries, when those clerks who managed England's national affairs increasingly recorded official matters in English, using features of their local spoken dialects—the language most natural to them. In the early fifteenth century, some who clerked in the royal administration in London came from the northeastern part of England, and in writing official court documents, mixed features of their native northern English in with London English. Others who wanted to participate in the affairs of state had to adopt the prestigious forms in their own writing, regardless of their own local dialects. Since London was the center of commercial affairs and literary production, as well as the seat of government, its dialect, infused with northernisms, became the standard for the literate Englishman. (Scotland developed its own standard.)

By the end of the sixteenth century, there had developed a form of early modern English that constituted the basis of our modern standard English.

> [The language of the poet should be] naturall, pure, and the most usuall of all his countrey: and for the same purpose rather that which is spoken in the kings Court, or in the good townes and Cities within the land, then in the marches and frontiers, or in port townes, . . . neither shall he follow the speach of a craftes

man or carter, or other of the inferiour sort, though he be inhabitant or bred in the best towne and Citie in this Realme, for such persons doe abuse good speaches by strange accents or ill shapen soundes, and false ortographie. But he shall follow generally the better brought up sort, such as the Greekes call **charientes** men civill and graciously behavioured and bred . . . ye shall therfore take the usuall speach of the Court, and that of London and the shires lying about London within lx. myles, and not much above. I say this but that in every shyre of England there be gentlemen and others that speake but specially write as good Southerne as we of Middlesex or Surrey do, but not the common people of every shire, to whom the gentlemen, and also their learned clarkes do for the most part condescend.
—George Puttenham's *The Arte of English Poesy,* 1589

It was at about this time too that there began to appear the first dictionaries and grammars of English. But for the next two hundred years, most grammarians wrote not to codify a standard English for speakers of nonprestigious dialects, but to help young students learn Latin. As a consequence, instead of trying to distinguish prestigious from less prestigious English, grammarians simply modeled grammars of English after Latin grammars, mapping the elaborate conjugations of Latin verb forms and paradigms of case inflections onto English parts of speech and inflections.

Not until the eighteenth century did grammarians begin to go substantially beyond the formal structure of Latin grammars to attend to particular differences that distinguished refined English from the English of the "vulgar." By that time there had developed enough desire for education and self-improvement for grammarians to make a profit not just from describing the basic structure of English for students of Latin, but from defining the niceties of educated English that, they claimed, distinguished the English of the cultivated from that of their inferiors. Between 1750 and 1775, almost as many first editions of grammar books were published as in all the years before. And by 1800 that total more than doubled again.

As grammars proliferated in the second half of the eighteenth century, each grammarian had somehow to distinguish his treatment of English from that of his competitors. Some offered new ways of teaching: some wrote for different audiences; others invented new names for the parts of speech. But another way that

they attempted to distinguish themselves was to codify—or invent—increasingly fine rules of usage. After all, no one sells more
books by offering fewer rules. It was during this period that we
began to accumulate the familiar rules about *lay* vs. *lie, different
to* vs. *different from,* split infinitives, and so forth.

However, in their zeal to describe the rules of "good" English,
these eighteenth-century grammarians failed to distinguish three
kinds of rules, a failure that afflicts most grammar books today.

Three Kinds of Rules

1. Some rules characterize the basic structure of English—articles precede nouns, verbs regularly precede objects, questions
begin with a verb or *who, when, why,* etc. No native speaker of
English has to think about these rules at all.

2. Some rules distinguish standard from nonstandard speech:
you was vs. *you were, He don't earn no money* vs. *he doesn't
earn any money.* The only writers and speakers who worry about
these rules are those upwardly mobile types who are striving to
join the educated class of writers and speakers. Those who already count themselves as educated think about these rules only
when they see or hear them violated.

3. Finally, some grammarians try to impose on those who already write educated standard English particular items of usage
that they think those educated writers should observe—don't
split infinitives; use *that,* not *which* for restrictive clauses; use
fewer, not *less* for countable nouns; don't use *hopefully* to mean
I hope. These are matters that few speakers and writers of nonstandard English worry about. They are, however, items about
which educated writers disagree. Indeed, the very fact that grammarians have for centuries been able to cite violations of these
rules in the writing of the educated is proof enough that for centuries many educated speakers and writers have ignored both the
grammarians and their rules. Which has been fortunate for the
grammarians, of course, because if those educated speakers had
all obeyed all the rules, the grammarians would have to had to
invent new ones.

Because so many grammarians have confounded these issues
for so long, the rules they have accumulated do not have equal
force. As a consequence, those among us who are insecure about
such matters or who profit from the insecurities of others, are

ready to treat with equal seriousness double negatives and a *like* for an *as*. For example:

> I see where the President said that, irregardless of what happens with the economy, he'll still be against tax increases, just like he has been in the past. He seems disinterested in what's happening in this country.

Would we expect someone who wrote that to be just as likely to go on like this?

> Me and my wife, we ain't sure he know the problems what troubles us. He don't seem to have no new ideas can help.

According to the editors of the *American Heritage Dictionary,* speakers who commit the "errors" in the first two sentences speak nonstandard English: *where* as a subordinating conjunction, *irregardless, like* for *as,* and *disinterested* for *uninterested.* If so, we would have to conclude that such speakers are equally likely to utter the second two sentences. Yet every point of questioned usage in those first two sentences occurs in the unselfconscious language of educated speakers (though usually only one to a sentence, of course). When it is called to their attention, they might correct a *like* for an *as*. On the other hand, it is most unlikely that any educated speaker would ever unselfconsciously utter or write any of the nonstandard usages in the second two sentences. The editors of *AHD* confused two kinds of usage— matters of dialect that distinguish educated from uneducated speakers and points of usage that grammarians have long criticized in the language of educated speakers.

Here is the heart of the problem: there are different kinds of rules.

1. Some rules account for the fundamental structure of English: *I saw a horse yesterday* vs. *Horse yesterday a saw I*.

2. Some rules distinguish the dialects of the educated and the uneducated: *knowed* vs. *knew, he don't have no idea* vs. *he doesn't have any idea.*

3. And some rules belong to that category of rules observed by some well-educated people, and ignored by others equally well-educated: split infinitives, *which* for *that,* etc.

Ordinarily, the first set of rules concerns us not at all. And if you are interested in this book, you probably aren't much concerned with the second set either. It is that third set of rules that concern—sometimes obsess—already competent but not entirely secure writers. They are the rules of usage out of which the Pop Grammarians have created their cottage industry.

The facts of the matter are these: a few especially fastidious writers and editors try to honor and enforce every rule of usage; most careful writers observe fewer; and there are a few writers and editors who know all the rules, but who also know that not all of them are worth observing and enforcing, and that they should observe other rules only on certain occasions.

What do those of us do who want to be careful writers?

We could adopt the worst-case policy: follow all the rules all the time because somewhere, sometime, someone might criticize us for something—beginning a sentence with *and* or ending it with *up*. And so, with a stack of grammar books and usage manuals close by, we scrutinize every sentence for all possible "errors," until we have learned the rules so well that we obey them without thought. That guarantees that we never offend anyone. But once we decide to follow all the rules, we deprive ourselves of stylistic flexibility. And sooner or later, we will begin to impose those rules—real or not—on others. After all, what good is learning a rule if all we can do is obey it?

But selective observance has its problems too, because that requires us to learn which rules to ignore, which always to observe, and which to observe in some circumstances and to ignore in others. This freedom to choose is further complicated by the fact that those who invoke every rule of grammar always seem to have the moral upper hand: they claim to be dedicated to precision, and they seem to know something about goodness that we don't. Conversely, if we know enough to dismiss some "rule" of grammar as folklore, we risk being judged permissive by those who are ignorant of the history of our language.

If we want to avoid being so labeled, but also want to do more than mindlessly follow all the rules, we have to know more about the rules than the rule-mongers do, even about those rules we decide to observe.

For example, some think that only the vulgarians at the gate use *impact* as a verb. If you choose to defer to that opinion, fine, but do so understanding the wholly idiosyncratic nature of that judgment. The word *impact* derives from the past participle of *impingere*, a Latin verb. Moreover, *impact* has been used as a verb since at least the early seventeenth century. (All this information is readily available in the unabridged *Oxford English Dictionary*). Finally, the word *compact* shares part of the same root, *compingere*, and no one I know objects to the verb *compact*. Certainly, one might, *ipse dixit*, continue to insist that *impact* should never be used as a verb because of the widespread animus against that usage, but like other such rules, the rule would be idiosyncratic, arbitrary, without historical or logical justification.

Others deplore the infelicity of those who would begin a sentence with *and* or *but*. On a matter of this kind, it is useful to advert to H. W. Fowler's *A Dictionary of Modern English Usage* (first edition, Oxford University Press, 1926; second edition, 1965), unquestionably the most conservative and most authoritative guide to correct British English usage (the preferred standard for most of the Pop Grammarians). The second edition was edited by Sir Ernest Gowers, who to Fowler's original entry on *and* added this: "That it is a solecism to begin a sentence with *and* is a faintly lingering superstition." And to the original entry for *but*, added ". . . see *and*." If we look through the prose of our most highly respected writers, we will find sentence after sentence beginning with *and* or *but*.

(Before you freely quote Fowler/Gowers on any of these matters, you might want to look at the entries under "illiteracies," "sturdy indefensibles," "superstitions," and "fetishes." Some of what I urge here is qualified there. An American reference work that summarizes most American authorities is Roy H. Copperud, *American Usage and Style: The Consensus* [Van Nostrand Reinhold Company, New York, 1980].)

We must reject as folklore any rule that is regularly ignored by otherwise careful, educated, and intelligent writers of first-rate prose. If reputable writers do not avoid ending their sentences with prepositions, then regardless of what some grammarians or editors would say, a preposition at the end of a sentence is not an error of usage—it is stylistically infelicitous on occasion, but not grammatically wrong. The standard adopted here is not that of Transcendental Correctness. It derives from the observable habits of those whom we could never accuse of having sloppy minds or of deliberately writing careless prose. To be sure, the best writers sometimes commit grammatical howlers. We can all slip up on the right number for a verb distant from its subject, and when someone calls such an error to our attention, we correct it. But when someone calls to my attention the fact that I begin sentences with *but,* I ask the person to name a writer who, in that person's opinion, is a nonpareil of linguistic decorum. We then begin leafing through something that person has published. Invariably, we find numerous instances of sentences beginning with *and* or *but,* along with a number of other so-called "errors of usage."

If any, at this point, throw up their hands in dismay and contempt, claiming that authorities like Fowler and all those otherwise excellent writers are still wrong, I can only ask that person what would count as evidence of his being mistaken, what would persuade him that he is in fact wrong? If that person can think of no evidence that would change his mind on these matters—not history, not the practice of good writers, not the opinion of those who are more informed than he, then we are debating not matters of usage but theology.

On the basis of this principle—what do the best writers not occasionally or mistakenly do, but regularly do—we can recognize four kinds of "rules" of usage.

Real Rules

The first—the most important—category of rules includes those whose violation would generally brand one as a writer of nonstandard English. Here are a few:

1. Double negatives: The engine had **hardly no** systematic care.
2. Nonstandard verb forms: They **knowed** that nothing would happen.
3. Double comparatives: This way is **more quicker.**
4. Some adjectives for adverbs: They did the work **real good.**
5. Pleonastic subjects: **These ideas they** need explanation.
6. Some incorrect pronouns: **Him and me** will study the problem.
7. Some subject-verb disagreements. **They was** ready to begin.

There are others, but they are so egregious that we all know they are never violated by educated writers. They is rules whose violations we instantly notes, but whose observance we entirely ignore.

Folklore

A second group of rules includes those whose observance we do not remark, and whose violation we do not remark either. In fact, these are not rules at all, but linguistic folklore, enforced by many editors and schoolteachers, but largely ignored by educated and careful writers.

What follows is based on a good deal of time spent reading prose that is carefully written and intended to be read no less carefully. I can assert only that the "rules" listed below are "violated" so consistently that, unless we are ready to indict for bad grammar just about every serious writer of modern English, we have to reject as misinformed anyone who would attempt to enforce them. I have selected the quotations that follow carefully. Each is from the prose of a writer of considerable intellectual and scholarly stature or who is widely known as an arch conservative on matters of usage (sometimes both). Should anyone retort that even if these writers are reputable, they can still make a mistake, I would respond that if we called these errors to the attention of their authors, they would certainly tell us to get lost.

1. Never begin a sentence with *because*. Allegedly, not this:

> Because we have access to so much historical fact, today we know a good deal about changes within the humanities which were not apparent to those of any age much before our own and which the individual scholar must constantly reflect on.
> —Walter Ong, S.J., "The Expanding Humanities and the Individual Scholar," *PMLA*

Some would prefer either of these:

> Since we have access to so much historical fact, today we know
> . . . We have access to much historical fact. Consequently we . . .

Though this particular proscription appears in no handbook of usage I know of, it has gained increasingly popular currency. It must stem from advice intended to avoid sentence fragments like this one.

The application was rejected. **Because the deadline had passed.**

When we add to this introductory *because-* clause a main clause and punctuate the two in a single sentence, the sentence is entirely correct:

Because the deadline had passed, the application was rejected.

An even more recent variation on this theme is the increasingly popular belief that we should not begin a sentence with a preposition either.

In the morning, everyone left.

This kind of folklore is almost certainly a consequence of over-generalizing the "rule" about *because*. Again, it is a "rule" with utterly no substance.

2. Never begin a sentence with a coordinating conjunction such as *and* or *but*. Allegedly, not this (a passage that violates the "rule" twice):

> **But,** it will be asked, is tact not an individual gift, therefore highly variable in its choices? **And** if that is so, what guidance can a manual offer, other than that of its author's prejudices—mere impressionism?
> —Wilson Follett, *Modern American Usage: A Guide,* edited and completed by Jacques Barzun et al.

As I said earlier, Gowers called this rule a "faintly lingering superstition." Just about any highly regarded writer of nonfictional prose begins sentences with *and* or *but,* some more than once a page.

3. When referring to an inanimate referent, use the relative pronoun *that*—not *which*—for restrictive clauses; use *which* for nonrestrictive clauses. Allegedly, not this:

> Next is a typical situation **which** a practiced writer corrects "for style" virtually by reflex action.
> —Jacques Barzun, *Simple and Direct,* p. 69.

Barzun had just the previous page written, "In conclusion, I recommend using **that** with defining clauses except when stylistic reasons interpose." (In this case, none of his stylistic reasons interposed.) When someone who offers up a rule immediately violates it, we know the rule has no force.

This rule first saw light of day in 1906, when Henry Fowler and his younger brother, Francis, presented it in *The King's English* (Oxford University Press; reprinted as an Oxford University Press paperback, 1973). They thought that the variation between *which* and *that* was messy, so they simply announced that henceforth we should (with some exceptions) restrict *which* to introducing nonrestrictive clauses, a rule with the full force of history and contemporary usage behind it:

> Abco ended its bankruptcy, **which** it had announced a year earlier.

But, according to the brothers Fowler, we should reserve *that* for *restrictive* clauses, a rule with no historical force or then-contemporary practice whatsoever.

> Abco developed a product **that** [not **which**] restored profitability.

Francis died in 1918, but Henry continued the family tradition with *A Dictionary of Modern English Usage.* In that landmark reference work, he spent more than a page discussing the fine points of this rule, and then, a bit wistfully perhaps, added (p. 635),

> Some there are who follow this principle now; but it would be idle to pretend that it is the practice either of most or of the best writers.

It is an observation that the editor of the second edition retained.

4. Don't use *which* or *this* to refer to a whole clause. Allegedly not this:

> Although the publishers have not yet destroyed the plates of the second edition of Merriam-Webster's unabridged dictionary, they do not plan to keep it in print, **which** is a pity.
> —Dwight Macdonald, "The String Untuned," *The New Yorker*

A purist would presumably prefer this:

> Although the publishers have not yet destroyed the plates . . . they do not plan to keep it in print, **a decision which** is a pity.

Occasionally, this kind of construction can be ambiguous. In the next example, is it the letter that makes me happy, or the fact that it was given to me?

> They gave me the letter, **which** made me happy.

A summative modifier would make one meaning unambiguous:

> They gave me a letter, **a thoughtful act that** made me happy.

When it is clear what the *which* refers to, this kind of reference is entirely acceptable.

5. Use *each other* to refer to two, *one another* to refer to three or more. Allegedly, not this:

> Now "society" is ever in search of novelty—and it is a limited body of well-to-do women and men of leisure. From the almost exclusive association of these persons with **each other,** there arises a kind of special vocabulary, which is constantly changing.
> —James B. Greenough and George L. Kittredge, *Words and Their Ways in English Speech*

Each other and *one another* are not invariably distinguished by all careful writers.

6. Use *between* with two, *among* with three or more. Allegedly not this:

> . . . government remained in the hands of fools and adventurers, foreigners and fanatics, who **between** them went near to wrecking the work of the Tudor monarchy.
> —George Macaulay Trevelyan, *A Shortened History of England*

We never use *among* with only two, but careful writers commonly use *between* with three or more.

7. Use *fewer* with nouns that you can count, *less* with quantities you cannot. Allegedly not this:

> I can remember no **less** than five occasions when the correspondence columns of *The Times* rocked with volleys of letters from the academic profession protesting that academic freedom is in danger and the future of scholarship threatened.
> —Noel Gilroy Annan, Lord Annan, "The Life of the Mind in British Universities Today," *ACLS Newsletter*

Although we never use *fewer* before uncountable singular nouns: *fewer sand,* educated writers do use *less* before countable plural nouns: *less problems.*

8. Use *due to* meaning 'because of' only in a phrase that modifies a noun, never in a phrase that modifies a verb. Allegedly not this:

> . . . cooperation between the Department of Economics and the Business School and between the Business School and the Law School will be much greater ten years from now than at present,

due to the personal relations of the younger men on the three
faculties.
—James Bryant Conant, *The President's Report: 1951–1952.*
Harvard University Press

There are several words some of whose particular usages are
proscribed by extremely conservative teachers and editors. But
most careful writers nevertheless use *since* with a meaning close
to 'we take for granted that the claim in this clause is true':

Since we agree on the matter, we need not discuss it further.

Careful writers use *while* with a meaning close to 'although what
follows in the next clause is the case right now, we can simultaneously assert a contradictory or qualifying claim':

While we agree on the main issues, we disagree on the next steps.

Careful writers use *alternative* to refer to one of three or more
choices; *anticipate* to mean 'expect'; *contact* as a general verb
meaning 'enter into communication with'. Though *data* and *media* as singulars are bêtes noires for some observers, they are used
as singular nouns by many careful writers, in the same way they
use *agenda* and *insignia*. (For most careful writers, *strata, errata,*
and *criteria* still seem to be plural.) *Infer* for *imply* and *disinterested* for *uninterested* are countenanced by some standard dictionaries whose editors base their decisions on the usage of
careful writers. Many teachers and editors strenuously disagree.

(A nice point about *disinterested:* Its original meaning was, in
fact, that of 'uninterested'. Only in the eighteenth century did it
begin to take on the meaning of 'impartial'. A careful writer today does not use *disinterested* for *uninterested,* of course. But
those who cite *disinterested* as an example of the imminent de-
mise of English might consider instead whether such a usage in
fact shows how resistant to change our language really is.)

On the most formal of occasions, occasions on which you
would want to avoid the slightest hint of offending those who
believe in all the rules, folklore or not, you might decide to observe all of these rules. In ordinary circumstances, though, these
"rules" are ignored by most careful writers, which is equivalent
to saying that these rules are not rules at all. If you adopt the
worst-case approach and observe them all, all the time—well, to
each his own. Private virtues are their own reward.

Optional Rules

These next rules complement the first group: For the most part, few readers will notice if you violate them. But when you observe them, you will signal a level of formality that few careful readers will miss.

1. "Never split an infinitive." Some purists would condemn Dwight Macdonald, a linguistic archconservative, for writing this:

> . . . one wonders why Dr. Gove and his editors did not think of labelling *knowed* as substandard right where it occurs, and one suspects that they wanted **to slightly conceal** the fact or at any rate to put off its exposure as long as decently possible.
> —"The String Untuned," *The New Yorker*

They would require this:

> . . . one wonders why Dr. Gove and his editors did not think of labelling *knowed* as substandard right where it occurs, and one suspects that they wanted **to conceal the fact slightly** or at any rate to put off its exposure as long as decently possible.

But the split infinitive is now so common among the very best writers that when we make an effort to avoid splitting it, we invite notice, whether we intend to or not.

2. "Use *shall* as the first person simple future, *will* for second and third person simple future; use *will* to mean strong intention in the first person, *shall* for second and third person." Some purists would condemn F. L. Lucas for writing this:

> I **will** end with two remarks by two wise old women of the civilized eighteenth century.
> —"What Is Style?" *Holiday*

They would demand:

> I *shall* end with two remarks by two wise old women of the civilized eighteenth century.

They would be mistaken to do so.

3. "Always use *whom* as the object of a verb or preposition." Purists would condemn William Zinsser for writing this:

> Soon after you confront this matter of preserving your identity, another question will occur to you: "**Who** am I writing for?"
> —*On Writing Well*

They would insist on:

> Soon after you confront this matter of preserving your identity, another question will occur to you: "For **whom** am I writing?"

Whom is a small but distinct flag of conscious correctness, especially when the *whom* is in fact wrong:

> We found a candidate *whom* we thought was most qualified.

The rule: The form of the pronoun depends on whether it is a subject or an object of its own clause. Since *who* is the subject of *was* in

> We found a candidate ↑ we thought **who** was most qualified.

who is the correct form, not *whom*. In this next example, *whom* is the object of *overlooked:*

> We found a candidate ↑ we thought we had overlooked. **whom**

If you are in doubt about the matter, try dropping the *who/ whom* altogether:

> We found a candidate we thought we had overlooked.

4. "Never end a sentence with a preposition." Purists, presumably, would condemn Sir Ernest Gowers for this:

> The peculiarities of legal English are often used as a stick to beat the official **with.**
> —*The Complete Plain Words*

And insist on this:

> The peculiarities of legal English are often used as a stick **with which** to beat the official.

The second is more formal than the first, but the first is still correct. In fact, whenever we move a preposition before its object, we make the sentence a bit more formal. And any obligatory *whom* after the preposition only compounds the formality. Compare:

> The man **with whom** I spoke was not the man **to whom** I had been referred.
> The man I spoke **with** was not the man I had been referred **to.**

5. "Do not use *whose* as the possessive pronoun for an inanimate referent." Purists would correct I. A. Richards for this:

> And, on other occasions, the meaning comes from other partly parallel uses, **whose** relevance we can feel, without necessarily being able to state it explicitly.
> —*The Philosophy of Rhetoric*

They would change it to this:

> And, on other occasions, the meaning comes from other partly parallel uses, the relevance **of which** we can feel, without necessarily being able to state it explicitly.

6. "Use *one* as a generalized pronoun instead of *you*." Purists would revise Monroe Beardsley's:

> When explicit meanings are wrongly combined, **you** get a logical fault (this is oversimplifying somewhat, but take it as a first approximation).
> —"Style and Good Style," *Reflections on High School English: NDEA Institute Lectures*, ed. Gary Tate

into the more stilted:

> When explicit meanings are wrongly combined, **one** gets a logical fault (this is oversimplifying somewhat, but **one** may take it as a first approximation).

7. "Do not refer to *one* with *he* or *his;* repeat *one*." Purists would deplore Theodore Bernstein's usage:

> Thus, unless one belongs to that tiny minority who can speak directly and beautifully, **one** should not write as **he** talks.
> —*The Careful Writer*

They would prefer the more formal:

> Thus, unless **one** belongs to that tiny minority who can speak directly and beautifully, **one** should not write as **one** talks.

8. "When expressing a contrary-to-fact statement, use the subjunctive form of the verb." Purists would deny H. W. Fowler this:

> Another suffix that is not a living one, but is sometimes treated as if it **was,** is *-al;* & . . . .
> —*A Dictionary of Modern English Usage*

They would insist upon:

> Another suffix that is not a living one, but is sometimes treated as
> if it were, is -al; & . . . .

As the English subjunctive quietly subsides into linguistic history,
it leaves a residue of forms infrequent enough to impart to a sentence a tone that is slightly archaic, and therefore formal. We
regularly use the simple past tense to express most subjunctives:

> If we **knew** what to do, we **would** do it.

Be is the problem: Strictly construed, the subjunctive demands
were, but *was* is gradually replacing it:

> If this **were** 1941, a loaf of bread would cost twenty cents.

> If this **was** 1941, a loaf of bread would cost twenty cents.

Certainly, when the occasion calls for sonorous formal English,
the wise writer chooses the formal usage. But in all these cases,
the writer *chooses.*

Special Formality

The list of items that create a special sense of formality might
include a few that don't involve disputed points of usage, but do
let you elevate your style a bit above the ordinary.

1. Negative inversion. Probably the most famous negative inversion is President John F. Kennedy's

> **Ask not** what your country can do for you, ask what you can do
> for your country.

Compare:

> Do not ask what your country can do for you, . . .

Negatives such as *rarely, never, not, only,* and so on, typically let
you put an auxiliary verb before its subject:

> **Never have** so many owed so much to so few.

> **Rarely do** we confront a situation such as this.

> **Only once has** this corporation failed to pay a dividend.

2. Conditional inversion. Instead of beginning a conditional
clause with *if,* begin it with *should, were,* or *had.* Compare:

If anyone should question the grounds on which this decision was made, we can point to centuries of tradition.

Should anyone question the grounds on which this decision was made, we can point to centuries of tradition.

If there had been any objections, they would have been met.

Had there been any objections, they would have been met.

If I were prepared to answer you now, I should do so happily.

Were I prepared to answer you now, I should do so happily.

3. Instead of *do not have to,* use *need not:*

You **don't have** to answer now.

You **need not** answer now.

4. Instead of *does not have* any, use *have no:*

The court **does not have** any precedent to follow.

The court **has no** precedent to follow.

Bêtes Noires

For some, one set of "rules" has become the object of particularly fierce attention. They are the rules that the Pop Grammarians endlessly rehearse as evidence that English is close to being a terminal case. Why they excite such intense feeling has no rational explanation, but they have become the symbolic flags around which those most intensely concerned with linguistic purity (whatever that may be) have tacitly agreed to rally. None of these "errors" interferes with clarity and concision; indeed, some of them let us save a word or two. But for some reason, they arouse such intense ire in some editors, teachers, and ordinary citizens that every writer should be aware of their special status. However real those feelings may be, though, we have to understand that these so-called rules are largely capricious, with no foundation in logic or linguistic efficiency.

1. Never use *like* for *as* or *as if.* Not this:

These operations failed **like** the earlier ones did.

But this:

These operations failed **as** the earlier ones did.

Like became a conjunction in the eighteenth century when writers began to drop the *as* from the conjunctive phrase *like as*, leaving just *like* to serve as the conjunction. This kind of semi-ellipsis is one of the most common kinds of linguistic change. It is worth noting, perhaps, that the editor of the second edition of Fowler deleted *like* for *as* from Fowler's list of "illiteracies" and moved it into the "sturdy indefensibles" category. The editor of the third edition will probably remove it altogether.

2. After *different* use *from*, never *to* or *than*. Not this:

> These numbers are **different than** the others.
> I must solve this problem **differently than** I did last year.

But this:

> These numbers are **different from** the others.
> I must solve this problem **differently from the way** I did last year.

This is one of those cases where ignoring the rule can save a few words.

3. Use *hopefully* only when the subject of the sentence is in fact hopeful. Not this:

> **Hopefully,** the matter will be resolved soon.

But this:

> **I hopefully say** that the matter will be resolved soon.

This rule has become so deeply entrenched in the minds of so many that it is impossible to convince them that it is entirely idiosyncratic. When used to introduce a sentence such as

> **Hopefully,** it will not rain tomorrow

hopefully refers to the feelings of the speaker:

> **I am hopeful when I say** it will not rain tomorrow.

It is parallel to introductory words such as *candidly, bluntly, seriously, frankly, honestly, sadly,* and *happily*:

> **Seriously,** you should be careful → **I am serious** when I say . . .

While no one condemns a speaker who uses one of these words to describe his attitude, many grammarians deplore the substantially analogous **hopefully**. Logic further requires that if we want to reject all introductory words that we think are "vague" or "unspecific," then we should reject all metadiscourse such as *to summarize, in conclusion, finally,* etc., because every one of those words and phrases also qualifies the voice of the writer: *I summarize, I conclude, I say finally.* But of course, logic has nothing to do with these points of usage.

4. Do not modify an absolute word such as *perfect, unique, final,* or *complete* with *very, rather, quite,* etc. Not this:

> We require a **more perfect** system.

(We might wonder what the Founding Fathers would have said to those who criticized "We the People of the United States, in order to form *a more perfect union* . . ." Perhaps a constitutional amendment is called for.)

5. Never use *finalize* to mean *finish, complete, end. Finalize* does not mean what any of those other words mean. *Finalize* means to clean up the last details of an extended project, a specific sense captured by no other word. Some may think *finalize* still smacks too much of the bureaucratic mind, an understandable objection. But we ought to not accept the argument that the word is unnecessary, or ugly because of the *-ize;* if we did, we would have to reject *nationalize, synthesize, rationalize, equalize,* along with hundreds of other commonly used words. In fact, critics of English have been objecting to *-ize* since the sixteenth century because they thought the Greek ending should not be combined with Latin, French, and Anglo-Saxon roots.

6. Never never use *irregardless* for *regardless.* Most object to the double negative of *ir—less.* It is probably a blend of *irrespective* and *regardless.* That putative history doesn't legitimize *irregardless* (or should I say, make it legitimate?). But it does make the form of the word explicable.

A Special Problem: Pronouns and Sexism

> We expect verbs to agree with their subjects. Not this:

> There **is** several **reasons** for this.

But this:

> There **are** several **reasons** for this.

So do we ordinarily expect pronouns to agree in number with their referents. Not this:

> The early **efforts** to oppose the building of a hydrogen bomb failed because **it** was not coordinated with the scientific and political communities. **No one** was willing to step forth and expose **themselves** to the anti-Communist hysteria unless **they** had the backing of others.

But this:

> The early **efforts** to oppose the building of a hydrogen bomb failed because **they** were not coordinated with the scientific and political communities. **No one** was willing to step forth and expose **himself** to the anti-Communist hysteria unless **he** had the backing of others.

There are two problems here. The first is whether to use a singular or plural pronoun when referring to a singular noun that is plural in meaning: *group, committee, staff, administration,* and so on. Some writers use a singular pronoun when the group acts as a single entity:

> The **committee** has met but has not yet made **its** decision.

But when the members of the group act individually, we always use a plural pronoun:

> The **committee** received the memo, but not all of **them** have read it.

These days we find the plural used in both senses.

The second problem is whether to use a masculine or a feminine pronoun to refer to indefinite pronouns like *someone, everyone, no one* and to nouns that do not indicate gender: *a teacher, a person, a student.*

> **Everyone** who spends four years in college realizes what a soft life **they** had only when **they** get a nine-to-five job, with no summer and Christmas vacations.
>
> When **a person** gets involved with drugs, no one can help **them** unless **they** want to help **themselves**.

In both cases, more formal usage requires the singular pronoun:

> **Everyone** who spends four years in college realizes what a soft life **he** had only when **he** gets a nine-to-five job, with no summer and Christmas vacations.
>
> When **a person** gets involved with drugs, no one can help **him** unless **he** wants to help **himself**.

But when we observe the formal rule, we raise another, thornier problem—the matter of sexist language.

Obviously, what we perceive to be our social responsibilities and the sensitivities of our audience must always come first: Many believe that we lose little, and gain much, by substituting *humankind* for *mankind, police officer* for *policeman, synthetic* for *man-made,* etc. (Those who ask whether we should also substitute *personhole cover* for *manhole cover,* or *person-in-the-moon* for *man-in-the-moon,* either miss the point, or are making a tendentious one.) And if we are writing for an audience that might judge our language sexist, then sheer common sense demands that we find ways to express our ideas in nonsexist ways, even at the cost of a little wordiness. We do no harm when we substitute for *The Dawn of Man* something like *The Dawn of Human Society,* and some good.

But a generic *he* is different: If we reject *he* as a generic pronoun because it is sexist, and *they* to refer to indefinite singulars because it is diffuse or potentially ambiguous (its formal "grammaticality" aside), we are left with either a clumsily intrusive *he or she* or an imperative to rewrite sentence after sentence in arbitrary and sometimes awkward ways.

Now, no one with even the dullest ear for style can choose the first alternative without flinching:

> When a writer does not consider the ethnicity of his or her readers, they may respond in ways he or she would not have anticipated to certain words that for him or her are entirely innocent of ethnic bias.

So we have to rewrite. We can begin by substituting something for the singular *his,* perhaps plurals:

> When a **writer** does not consider the ethnicity of **his** readers . . .
>
> When **writers** do not consider the ethnicity of **their** readers . . .

We can also try passives, nominalizations, and other phrases that let us drop pronouns altogether:

> **Failure to consider** a reader's ethnic background may result in an **unexpected response** to certain words that the writer considers entirely innocent of ethnic bias.

When it's appropriate, we can always try switching the pronoun from a third person *he* to a second person *you* or a first person *we:*

> If **we** do not consider the ethnic background of **our** readers, **they** may respond in ways **we** would not expect to certain words that to **us** are entirely innocent of ethnic bias.

Finally, we can use *she* where we might otherwise use a *he,* as we have done in this book.

Each of us has to decide whether the social consequences of a sexist *he* justify the effort required to avoid it and the occasionally graceless or even diffuse style that such an effort can produce. No one committed to writing the clearest, most fluent and precise prose can fail to recognize the value of a generic *he:* It lets us begin a sentence briskly and smoothly; it lets us assign to a verb specific agency; it lets us avoid ambiguity, diffuseness, and abstraction.

But for the kind of writing that most of us do, nuances of phrasing and cadence so fine may be less important than the social value of unqualified nonsexist language. Its cost is a moment's thought and an occasionally self-conscious sentence. That cost is slight; the benefit is greater.

Precision

You may assign some of these items of usage to categories different from those I have suggested. Some readers would add others. And some would insist that they all belong in that first category of rules, those rules whose observance distinguishes civilized speakers and writers of standard English from those who are not. If we don't respect all of these rules all the time, they argue, we begin the slide down the slippery slope into national inarticulateness.

The impulse to regulate—and by regulating fix—language has a long tradition, not only in the English-speaking world, but in literate cultures everywhere. It is an impulse usually rooted in the fear that when language changes, it is usually for the worse; that if language changes too quickly, we will eventually lose touch with our written tradition. The English of Shakespeare and Dryden will eventually become as difficult as Chaucer is for most of us, and as foreign as *Beowulf* is for us all.

There are other fears, less clearly articulated perhaps, but still real. Some fear the slippery slope: If we give up on *hopefully* and *between you and I,* then we give up all standards, all care, and the language will degenerate. A commonly cited example of such a threatening change is a point of usage that some critics think is a recent barbarism: *between you and I*. Unchecked, they believe, this error will eventually threaten the integrity of the whole language. When we have the opportunity and the standing to point out an unfortunate *I* for a *me*, we probably ought to. But we ought not think that, if we leave it uncorrected, we invite linguistic chaos. Here is an interesting observation about that error:

> In the first Edition, of this work, I had used the phrase *between you and I*, which tho[ugh] it must be confessed to be ungrammatical, is yet almost universally used in familiar conversation. (p. 67)

This was written by Archibald Campbell in the second edition of his *Lexiphanes*, published in 1767. For almost two-and-a-quarter centuries, then, *between you and I* has been a common locution, yet our system of pronouns seems to have survived largely unscathed. Again, I am not arguing in favor of *between you and I*. I am pointing out only that an error widely abused as a sign of our imminent linguistic decline has in fact been around for a long time, in wide usage, and so far, nothing seems to have happened to the rest of the language. We can agree to correct it, but we ought not try to cite it as evidence of the imminent decline of Western Linguistic Values.

Another reason we take all this so seriously is that we invest a great deal of effort in learning our standard forms of speech, and then in mastering the fine points that, we are told, distinguish careful, responsible English from the language of those who are crude, careless, and threatening. After investing so much time learning so many idiosyncratic points of usage (particularly spelling), we are hardly going to accept the language of those who did not similarly submit themselves to the discipline of spelling tests, parsing drills, and diagramming exercises. As much as we might fear for our language, we fear as much for the social return on our investment.

We have to put this matter of precision more precisely: We want to be grammatically correct. But if we include in our definition of correct both what is true and what is folklore, we risk missing what is important—that which makes prose turgid or concise, confusing or clear. We do not serve the end of clear, readable prose by getting straight all the *which*es and *that*s, by mending our split infinitives, by eradicating every *finalize* and *hopefully*. Too many of those who obsess on the trivia do not know how to deal with the more serious matters of clumsiness and imprecision. It is those who let clumsy and imprecise language go unnoticed, or if noticed unrevised, that risk letting clumsy and imprecise prose become the accepted standard. And when that happens, clumsy and imprecise thinking will lag not far behind. *That* is a matter worth some passion.

All of us who are committed to excellence in prose have a common end: a style that communicates effectively, even elegantly. That style, by and large, is one that is readable, precise, and forceful. Some believe that we can achieve that end only if we include in our definition of precision a precise adherence to all the rules of usage. Others do not. Wherever you take your stand, keep this in mind: A writer who observes every rule can still write wretched prose. And some of the most lucid, precise, and forceful prose is written by those for whom some of these rules have no standing whatsoever.

Because the finer points of English usage are idiosyncratic, individual, unpredictable, I can offer no broad generalizations, no global principles by which to decide any given item. Indeed, if usage did submit to logical analysis, to systematic analogy, usage would be no issue, for as we have seen, most "errors" of usage occur when a speaker or writer extends a regularity too far. The social utility of idiosyncratic rules is precisely in their idiosyncrasy. It guarantees that they will be mastered only by those with the time and desire to do so.

Finally, I suspect, most of us choose among these items not because we believe that we are defending the integrity of the English language or the quality of our culture, but because we want to assert our own personal style. Some of us are straightforward and plainspeaking; others take pleasure in a bit of elegance, in a flash of fastidiously self-conscious "class." The *shall*s and the *will*s, the *who*s and the *whom*s, the self-consciously unsplit infinitives—they are the small choices that let those among us who wish to do so express their refined sense of linguistic decorum, a decorum that many believe testifies to their linguistic precision. It is an impulse we ought not scorn, when it is informed and thoughtful.

Those writers whose prose we take most seriously set the standard for the rest of us. But those who manage the writing of others less eminent have an even greater responsibility. By their attention, knowledge, and skill, they directly determine the quality of our national discourse, not just as it appears in our national journals, but in the course of our daily professional lives. An improvement in the quality of our most mundane prose will make the biggest difference in the quality of our lives.

This book, we hope, will contribute to that improvement, perhaps to this ideal articulated by Alfred North Whitehead:

> Finally, there should grow the most austere of all mental qualities; I mean the sense for style. It is an aesthetic sense, based on admiration for the direct attainment of a foreseen end, simply and without waste. Style in art, style in literature, style in science, style in logic, style in practical execution have fundamentally the same aesthetic qualities, namely, attainment and restraint. The love of a subject in itself and for itself, where it is not the sleepy pleasure of pacing a mental quarterdeck, is the love of style as manifested in that study. Here we are brought back to the position from which we started, the utility of education. Style, in its finest sense, is the last acquirement of the educated mind; it is also the most useful. It pervades the whole being. The administrator with a sense for style hates waste; the engineer with a sense for style economizes his material; the artisan with a sense for style prefers good work. Style is the ultimate morality of mind.[14]

Notes

1. Alex Inkeles and Larry Sirowy, "Convergence in Education," *Social Forces* 62, no. 2 (1983).

2. Second College ed. New York: Simon and Schuster, 1980.

3. "Fenimore Cooper's Literary Offences," *North American Review*, July 1895.

4. New York, 1973, p. xv.

5. Cambridge, Mass.: MIT Press, 1984, p. 153.

6. John P. Gilbert, Bucknam McPeek, and Frederick Mosteller, "Statistics and Ethics in Surgery and Anesthesia," *Science* 198 (November 18, 1977): 684–89.

7. *The White Album,* pp. 41–42. New York: Simon and Schuster, 1979.

8. New York: Simon and Schuster, 1981, pp. 116–17.

9. London: A. Lane, 1984, p. 304.

10. Stanford University Press, 1988, p. 140.

11. Trans. Gayatri Chakravorty Spivak. Baltimore: The Johns Hopkins University Press, 1976, p. 6.

12. Boston: Little, Brown, 1967, pp. 231–32.

13. In *Thought and Object: Essays on Intentionality,* ed. Andrew Woodfield. Oxford, Clarendon Press, 1982, p. 62.

14. From "The Aims of Education" in *The Aims of Education and Other Essays* by Alfred North Whitehead. New York: Macmillan, 1929.

Acknowledgments

Index